KING
OF THE
BENIGHTED

King of the Benighted

Manuchehr Irani

Translated from the Persian by
Abbas Milani

Mage Publishers
Washington, D.C.

This first edition of *King of the Benighted* is limited to 975 copies numbered
1 to 975. The front jacket illustration is Bahram Gur with the Indian Princess
in the Black Pavilion from the Khamsa of Nizami probably from the Qazwin
School circa 1590 courtesy of the Arthur M. Sackler Gallery, Smithsonian
Institution, Washington DC. The back jacket illustration is an earlier
painting circa 1445 from the Tabriz School. The volume
has been printed and bound by Cushing-Malloy,
Ann Arbor, Michigan, in the year
1990. This copy is
number

755

Copyright© 1990 Mage Publishers, Inc.

Library of Congress Cataloging-in-Publication Data
Irani, Manuchehr
[Shāh-i Siyāh Pūshān. English]
King of the Benighted: a novella by Manuchehr Irani
Translated by Abbas Milani
I. Milani, Abbas.
II. Nizāmì Ganjavì, 1140 or 41-1202 or 3. Haft Paykar. Selections.
III. Title.
PK6561.I64S513 1990 891'.5533—dc20 90-5609

ISBN 0-934211-26-4

Contents

INTRODUCTION

At a time when the world has just celebrated the end of a decade marked with momentous change, it would seem inappropriate to speak of *The Demonic Decade*—the title the poet protagonist of *King of the Benighted* has bestowed upon a collection of his own poems. But his perspective is that of an Iranian who witnessed the brutal end of another era in 1979.

If we expect "The Demonic Decade" to set the tone of this novella, we are in for a surprise. *King of the Benighted* is not a litany of shattered ideals; it is a startling and at times ironic self-examination which never loses sight of the absurd and the humorous.

Led away to interrogation, the hero is grateful for small mercies: "So long as they hit with a book and on his head, then there is something to rejoice for." Political commitment has given way to personal obsession. Will all of his books fit into the few boxes the interrogators have brought? Will they take away his precious copy of Nizami's thirteenth-century poem? Will the cracked wing of the plaster angel, standing in his garden, survive the winter?

Those seeking the definitive symbolic meaning of every

utterance made by the anonymous narrator will have their expectations thwarted at every turn. Like the thirteenth-century poem on which *King of the Benighted* is superimposed, this novella works on many levels. The poet's remarks about Nizami's *The Black Dome* are an apt description of the way in which his own novella should be read: "Well, that was the story. That is what he read. What counts is the interpretation. It has to be an inner experience, everyone must go through it."

The "inner" journey upon which the readers are required to embark is not unlike the one the king undertakes in *The Black Dome*. He sets out to learn why everyone is dressed in black in the City of the Bedazzled. He discovers the secret, only to emerge in mourning.

Should you want to know why Iran has become a nation of mourners, you might follow the poet where he has gone. Like the king in Nizami's poem, you yourself may become ebony-clad. But, like the poet of *King of the Benighted*, while donning the obligatory *black* of that land, you might escape the worst and emerge with a head of *white* hair. In the end, you will be at once benighted and bedazzled.

All along the journey, illusions are shed and resolutions made. The wisdom at which the poet arrives while in prison is that he has indeed missed out on a decade. As he says to his cellmate: "I've been cheated. For about ten years, my only audience has been people like you. Now, I realize I haven't written anything for a man in his forties, or even for myself."

With this declaration, the poet catapults his generation into a new literary era—one marked by an abrupt break with *The Demonic Decade*. He sees no point in writing about death, denouncing regimes, and spurring others to political action. For the anonymous hero of *King of the Benighted*, this is no time to lament, but a new chance at regeneration. This Iranian poet is, in spite of the isolation he suffers, very much part of the new spirit sweeping the world.

The final irony with which the poet is faced is that the renewal he envisions has to be transported outside his native land. But, after all, Nizami's King also had to travel to China to find the City of the Bedazzled.

NASRIN RAHIMIEH
University of Alberta
Edmonton, Canada

PROLOGUE

THE BLACK DOME

The Black Dome is part of a longer poem called *Haft Peykar* (Seven Beauties) by the Persian poet Nizami of Ganja (1141-1203). The seven beauties refer to seven portraits of daughters of different kings from the Raj of India and the Khaghan of China to the Shah of Kharazm and the king of the West, or "Sunset-land." When Bahram, the Sassanian King, discovers these portraits, he falls in love with them, and, upon succeeding to the throne vacated by the death of his father Yazdigird, he marries all seven princesses. They represent the climes into which the habitable world is divided and are lodged in separate symbolically colored palaces, beginning with the black and ending with the white. Bahram then visits them on seven successive days. Here is the story of the first night.

On Saturday, Bahram, dressed in black from head to foot, went to the Black Dome where his bride, the daughter of the Raj of India, lived. He asked the Princess to tell him a story and she, with her head cast down, said:

When I was a child, a pious and compassionate woman visited our house once a month, and she always wore black. After our many persistent inquiries, she finally gave in and told us the secret of her unusual attire.

When I was young, the woman said, I was servant to a mighty king in whose land sheep and wolves lived in security. Yet fate had it that he would become *King of the Benighted* and the story I'll tell you is how he came to wear black for the rest of his life.

He was a benevolent king with an insatiable desire to know the ways and the wonders of the world. At his command, a house was set up where all visitors to the land enjoyed the fruits of his hospitality; and then the king, with his keen and curious mind, inquired from each visitor about his homeland, his travels, his plans and adventures. Thus, the king spent his days and years. As men search for precious stones, he sought to collect tales about other men and their lives. The richer his collection became, the hungrier he was to learn more.

But suddenly the king vanished. Like the mythical bird Simurg, he too seemed to have disappeared from our midst. A long time passed and then one day the king, completely dressed in black, again ascended his throne.

One night, as I was tending to his needs, he began to lament the turns of his fortune. I sought the secret of his sorrow and this is the story he recounted:

You know of my habit of entertaining visitors to my land. From each I would ask about their cities and its wonders. One day a wanderer arrived dressed in black. I asked about his peculiar attire. He asked me to relinquish my inquiry, reminding me that no one has ever learned the secret of Simurg. The more I persevered, the more he persisted in his silence. "Only the ebony-clad can grasp the essence of this blackness," he said.

Yet I persisted and he finally said:

There is a beautiful city in China called the City of the Bedazzled. There everyone is in mourning. The wanderer then refused to utter another word and soon disappeared.

Amused by this tale, I resolved to solve the mystery of the city. Yet nobody seemed to know anything about the place. Thus, I temporarily relinquished my throne, and, taking some jewels with me, I set out to seek that mysterious city.

And indeed a beautiful city it was. Its inhabitants, all dressed in black, had faces glowing white as a moon. For a year I wandered through the city in search of the answer. Everyone seemed to know the answer, yet no one wished to talk. Finally, I befriended a noble-hearted butcher. Many a gift I gave him. Then one day, assured of his friendship, I told him about how I had left my throne to find out why these people are so grieved and always in black.

"An impudent question you've asked," he said, "but I will give you what answer I have."

That night he took me to a ruin outside the city. There, waited a basket, fastened to a rope. "Sit in this basket," he said, "and then you will know why we are so grieved and always dressed in black." Once I was in the basket, by some magic, the rope fastened around my neck, as it fastens around the body of a captive, and then the basket took to the air.

A tower, rising to the moon, soon came in view and there the basket landed. I, out of fear and frustration, closed my eyes. Soon, a bird as big as a mountain perched nearby. Only a few moments had passed when the bird fell asleep and I, rueing my trust in the butcher, resolved to cling to the bird and let it take me where it might.

Soon after the bird awakened, we flew high and away on a long journey, descending near a beautiful prairie. Flowers of every color adorned the land. Hyacinths, carnations, jasmine, and roses. Cedars lined the rivers that silently traveled through the prairie.

Overjoyed at the sight of such heavenly comforts, I wandered amongst the wilderness, napping occasionally and indulging in revelry.

A gentle wind awoke and caressed me; a spring cloud, brought along by the wind, sprayed a little rain, cool as pearls, over leaves and grass. No sooner had it ceased than something new astounded me. From afar I noticed a gleam of light approaching quickly. A long procession moved toward me in which single figures became distinguishable—they were girls, all of them, each one of such radiant beauty that I forgot the world and myself. They looked like enchanted moving blossoms wrapped in silk, their arms caressingly covered by golden lace. Behind the veil of lighted candles which they held in their henna-colored fingers, their lips smiled enticingly. And finally the Queen, or I should say the sun at midnight, appeared and ascended the throne.

A few minutes elapsed and then she said, "It seems to me someone, an earthling maybe, is here," and then she ordered one of the fairies to fetch whomever she found. The fairy came toward me and gently invited me to come before the Queen.

Once near the throne, I kissed the earth. She, however, invited me to ascend the throne and sit at her side. I refused, submitting that such a noble and lofty place befitted not I but Solomon. Yet she beckoned me on to her side, endearing me as an honorable guest.

An attendant gently took my hand and led me closer to her throne, where I was immediately enthralled by her beauty. All sorts of libations and delicacies were brought. Minstrels followed the feast as the cup bearer made the rounds and filled everyone's cup to the brim.

I, emboldened by the wine and encouraged by the Queen's affectionate and enticing gestures, ventured many a kiss upon her. Finally, I asked her name. "My father called me the 'Beautiful Turkish Raider',"she said. Surprised by the coincidence, I responded that I, too, but for different reasons, was called a Turkish Raider. And then I invited her to a feast of love to complement our feast of wine. The glow in her eyes encouraged me to persist. But when I embraced her more passionately, she said, "Tonight, with kisses be content, and to quell the fire of your passion, take a girl of your choice." Bewildered as I was, the Queen beckoned one of the fairies and she led me to a chamber. There I laid my head upon a pillow and then clasped that beauty tightly to my breast and deflowered the rose of her beautiful garden.

At the break of the dawn, she prepared me a bath, of a heavenly fragrance and when I rose to dress, I found myself alone. I wandered into the garden and slept the day away in a corner bedded by rose petals and full of flowers in bloom.

When I awoke, the dark veil of the night had already spread upon the sky and as I sat up, the fairies reappeared and repeated what they had done the night before.

The Fairy Queen, fresh as the first day of spring, soon reascended her throne and again invited me to her side. The feast of last night, replete with exquisite wines and rare morsels, along with generous cup bearers and gorgeous dancing girls, was all there again, and the Queen was even more endearing than the first night. The maidens left us alone in our embrace and again the passions of her body and warmth of the wine enticed me to fondle a beautiful lock of her hair. Finally, when I moved to engulf myself in her, she again counseled patience and warned against perfidy. "I, ever thirsty, and you so delicious a water, why all such reticence?" I asked. "Tonight with kisses be content" she responded, and once again I spent that most intimate hour of the night not with her but with a surrogate.

And so it was for twenty-nine days and nights. I detested the long days and anxiously awaited the nights.

On the thirtieth night, the Queen and her retinue returned, lighting up the ebony colored prairie. Once again she beckoned me to her side and thus the joyous feast began anew. Soon, passion broke through all shackles with which I had tried to enchain it, and my hands, spurred by powers beyond my control, searchingly sought the most intimate of her treasures. Composed and compassionate, the Queen took my hands away and while kissing them, again implored me to have patience, consoling me with a reminder that only through patience shall I taste the fruits of the tree that is already mine.

Ravaged by desire I, in anguish, told my sun-faced beauty that patience can no longer rein in my passion.

The Queen responded, "The treasure you so deeply seek is

already yours; you wish to have it too early; wait and in due time it shall be yours."

"You expect the impossible." I said. "To be so near a treasure and yet refrain from possessing it is beyond my powers."

Imploring to my reason, this time she asked me to wait only till tomorrow, adding, "a night is not a year," and again suggesting that I calm myself in the company of one of her moon-faced beauties.

But her appeals to reason were of little avail. Indeed, they only fueled the fire of my passion; thus, oblivious to her pleas, I persisted in my quest to open her ruby-like treasure.

The Queen, recognizing that I could no longer be restrained, finally said, "Close your eyes for a moment, then you can taste the flower of my treasure."

Enticed by her suggestion and anxious for eternal bliss, I obeyed and closed my eyes. A minute passed. "Now open your eyes," she said.

I opened them only to find myself alone, in a frightening darkness, dangling in a descending basket.

My friend, ebony-clad, awaited at the foot of the tower. He embraced me and said, "Now you know why we are dressed in black. Mere words could never convey the cause of our plight."

I could only agree and simply asked him to fetch me some black garments. I wore them in mourning of the lost ideal; an ideal lost in callow hope.

Thus ended the king's tale. I, his humble servant, in compassion also wore black, for amongst the seven colors of the seven heavens, none is as great as black.

King of the Benighted

*A*gain this morning as he opened his eyes, he saw that Farkhondeh's mother was not staring or even glancing furtively, as the living do, but looking at him from the depth of the two glazed eyes that were left of her in the picture, with that gray and limpid color of a much reprinted black and white photograph. Her hair was disheveled, and she was looking at him. She had said, "What's the meaning of it all?"

By the bedside, standing there, perhaps on top of the dressing table, and frameless, between the two silvery hooks of a light wooden base, in such a way that it occasionally seemed to quiver.

The picture had been taken years ago, when Farkhondeh was probably only five or six; it had stood there on the dressing table for fifteen or sixteen years. When Grandfather died, she put his picture in the lower corner of the mirror. When her brother disappeared (they still say he might be a prisoner of war, although there has been no word of him for about a year), his picture was added to the other two. It is in the upper right hand corner of the mirror. The nice thing about Grandfather's picture is that it doesn't look at him, although you can see his eyes. When Grandfather died, he was already blind, with dark glasses. His eyes, or whatever is left of them in the photogtaph, don't say anything.

He turned his back to the picture, and said, "What a grave-yard they've made."

He rolled over. Maybe it was all because of the *Hejleh*[1] he saw on the street corner yesterday afternoon. A martyred soldier or a revolutionary guard. He no longer remembered names. It might still be there. A little boy, plate in hand, was giving out dates as alms. All around the glittering *Hejleh* hung pictures of the young martyr. Young, smiling, beardless. Per-haps he had been only old enough to have down on his face. He must have just shaved to leave a hint of beard blossom on his countenance. That was it. Two other young men, com-pletely dressed in black, sat on the front step of the closed store. They were talking. That's it. A young man, barely bearded, and dressed in black was looking at him.

When the phone rang, he didn't answer, yet he remembered. How could he have forgotten? Well, that's how things are, first the news on the phone, then maybe a memorial service,

---

1. *Hejleh* literally means "bridal-chamber." In the vernacular, it has come to refer to a large crown-like construction, adorned with lights, mirrors and candles; it is placed in front of houses mourning the loss of a young unmarried man.

or even a visit to the cemetery, and that is it. He had seen Amir Khan[2] only three or at most four times. He was probably sixty some years old, that is if we assume he began fighting around 1939, probably his freshman year in college. Now, he has died of a stroke. They had given him the news on the phone, before he could go to his hideaway. It had been Pari's husband. He had answered, "Of course, it is our duty."

And then, when he had hung up, he thought, these days, even young ones die of heart attacks. This one had died of a stroke. Amir Khan himself used to say, "I've had enough."

Maybe that's why he wouldn't talk anymore. How much he had tried to get him to talk. It is no joke. He had been fighting from 1939 or 1941 at the latest, all the way through 1946, and the Azerbaijan episode; 1948 was the year when the party was declared illegal, and then, it was August nineteenth 1953 when he went underground, for two years and a month, then finally, he turned himself in. For a few years, he was imprisoned in the military garrison, and then, it was

---

2. Amir Khan was obviously a member of the Tudeh Party, and many of the historical dates referred to in the next few paragraphs are all moments in the history of that party.

The Tudeh Party was founded in October of 1941 under the auspices of the Soviet Union, then occupying parts of Iran. It has since remained a religiously faithful supporter of the Soviet Union.

Toward the end of the war, Stalin toyed with the idea of dismembering some regions of Iran. By exploiting nationalist sentiments, he helped create the Democratic Party of Azerbaijan that ostensibly fought for national autonomy in the Turkish-speaking state of Azerbaijan. Under pressures brought by the U.S. government, and as a consequence of a promise of oil concessions by the then acting Iranian prime minister, the Soviets stopped their support of the Democratic Party, hence allowing the Iranian government to reestablish its authority over the region. The Tudeh Party remained a faithful, but often embarrassed supporter of all the ominous Soviet moves in the Azerbaijan Episode.

In the post-war years, the Tudeh Party became the most organized and powerful political party in Iranian politics. Many of the intellectuals were drawn to the party.

In 1948, after a failed assassination attempt against the Shah, the party was declared

Ghezel Ghale.[3] Ghezel Ghale has been demolished, as if it had never been there, or that the old man had never served any time in it. In the place of the old prison cells are fruit and vegetable kiosks. Pari's husband had said, "He had become completely paralyzed." Yet, he had been conscious enough to say, "Son, I've had enough."

Where was he to get a black shirt? That's necessary. How long can one put it off? He must also have a black suit, black from head to toe.

Again, the phone. A wrong number. Maybe it was the one who calls and remains silent; only the sound of his inhaling or exhaling can be heard. His daughters had left. His wife had left too. She had written his chores of the day on a slip now hanging from a clip: "Buy fruit. Turnips two kilos. Out of turmeric. Buy bread, if you have time. Yogurt, if you can find it. Lunch is in the refrigerator." She even signs it.

In the afternoon, he must attend the old man's memorial—the Third Day memorial. He used to say: "This time I wasn't fooled. I knew every one of them." He was referring to the

---

illegal, but it continued its activity through the many front organizations it had created.

In 1951 Mossadeq was elected prime minister and went on to nationalize the Iranian oil industry, leading to a major confrontation with England and ultimately the United States.

In August 1953, a coup, masterminded by the C.I.A. and British Intelligence and essentially actualized by notorious characters such as *Shaban The Brainless*, overthrew the government of Mossadeq.

The Tudeh Party, in spite of its popular base and a large clandestine network of sympathetic army officers, remained more or less passive. The ensuing political oppression destroyed nearly all of the Tudeh Party's organization in Iran. Much of the top leadership fled to Eastern Europe.

3. Ghezel Ghale was a heinous building in the heart of Tehran where, between the forties and the sixties, most of the political prisoners were held, interrogated, and often tortured.

days after 1978.[4] It was as if he were saying, "I raised them myself." His children were all now of independent means. Occasionally, he would read; every few months he would visit one of the children. He died in Shiraz. Pari's husband broke the news on the phone.

They were knocking at the door. Yet there was electricity. He checked it by turning the light on. A beggar perhaps; so many of them around these days. He poured himself a cup of tea. Again, a knocking at the door and a ringing of the bell. Clearly it was a beggar. He sweetened his tea. He usually ate only a couple of bites, then smoked a cigarette. This was the minimum preparation needed to get him ready for working. The knocking stopped. The old man had told Pari: "I don't want to lie around like a corpse." Maybe what had happened was exactly what he had in mind: from the neck down, paralyzed. He had said to his niece, "End it."

Pari is now probably completely dressed in black. With the mourning veil they look more beautiful. Usually they give you a pill. Maybe they even give you strong injections of sedative for a few hours. Perhaps Shiraz too has a place like Behesht-e Zahra,[5] with its endless rows of uniform gravestones. At least nowadays they let you set up a pedestal with a picture on it. But maybe the old way with no adornments was better; rows and rows, as far as the eye could see, all neatly arranged, all

---

4. In 1978, with the rise of the revolutionary movement in Iran, the leadership of the Tudeh Party returned home and attempted to reorganize the old cadres that had remained in Iran. Some responded positively to this invitation. Many, like Amir Khan, chose to ignore it.

5. Behesht-e Zahra is a large cemetery outside Tehran. Many of those killed in war and in the revolution are buried there.

the way to the wall or to the awaiting desert. The *Hejleh* stands in the street only a few days. Then the only thing that remains is the headstone. The picture was black and white, but the eyes seemed to be a different hue. He had a smile, something between shame and fear of the photographer, or of the picture not turning out right. Will they too, like Farkhondeh, place the picture in the corner of a mirror on their dressing table? Or maybe they'll frame it and hang it on the wall? No choice. He must buy a black shirt. The phone rang again, and again it was he, or maybe the subject of another picture for another *Hejleh*. Before noon he wouldn't answer any calls. That was his routine.

When he lit his cigarette, he again heard knocking at the door. They were banging on it with fists. Let them bang! Acquaintances knew, so did most of his friends. The girls had their own key; Farkhondeh too. These few hours were all he had to himself. That was their implicit agreement. It could not be one of them.

And again, there were the blank sheets of paper, present even in his dreams. Sometimes, even when he scribbled them black, they remained blank. His wrists would ache, but not a single word, not even a dot would imprint itself upon the perennial blankness. Those times, those days . . . what happened to them? He would write on anything he could get his hands on. From collated pieces of paper, cut-out corners of newspaper, backs of cigarette boxes, margins of books he had read, he would connect not only moments and hours, but days, like running after a kite with a lingering tail, blowing away to that distant blue in the sky, over the trees and the minarets and sometimes even onto the pavement, and into the puddle he had not noticed while writing and stepped into, ankle deep. He wouldn't even notice the puddle. Afterward, on arrival at a cafe, he would know from his wet socks and the water in his shoes, and then, only after he had tucked away the piece of paper, squarely folded, in his pocket. That is probably how it passed, how he arrived at this moment, these few hours, this vacuity and solitude that would be his until his daughters returned from school at noon, and if he decided to ignore the daily chores, it will be him and the papers. Those words, where did they come from? He now knew they were simply an effervescence. Yet, those days were better, and not now when he would obsessively hesitate over every word, and then, beyond these three or four hours, some people might, once in a long while, read a poem of his and probably think to themselves: "Well, at least he's still around." Some of his poems can't even be published. But they had published them abroad, a selection of works from these years. Just last year, he told them to name it *The Demonic Decade*. Now, perhaps those who had fled the country, lest they have to hang a picture of their son on one of these *Hejlehs*, would place his book, unread by them and unseen by himself, on their shelves. But what is the use, after all? These words couldn't solve anything. He had only rhymed them, arranged them in lines, and occasionally adorned them with metaphors. No, the five hairy, clawed fingers that had dug deep into his neck would not so easily let go of him. They, and everyone else, can see the long line that comes running every night, flagellating their chests, red and green flags in hand, a bandana, surely red around the forehead, running only to return as a picture on a street corner. He was really handsome, with a cleft in his chin. He was looking at him. Sometimes they would paint the wall around the house of the family that had lost a son and write their slogans on them. They even decorate them with lights.

Amir Khan used to say: "I was devastated, believe me. He was my eldest grandson. They just gave us the news, nothing else. Then a group of women, having barely knocked at the door, poured in. They began wailing. They even flagellated. They wouldn't let us, we who were supposedly the family of the deceased, do a thing. One of them went into the kitchen and took charge of the tea and the hooka and every other goddamned thing. One of them began reciting elegies for women. Two sat on the two sides of Ashkan's mother, like so. Later a few men came on motorcycles, wearing trench coats, supposedly to take care of me. They were trying to console me. They stayed for three days. I couldn't take it, so out I went."

They get sugar, tea, and even meat and beans from the mosque. This company of mourners, dressed in black, do the cooking, serve the guests, and even do the sobbing, only, of course, upon hearing elegies for Ghasem and Ali Akbar Hossein.[6] Only at this point can the family of the martyr weep. He had to buy a black shirt. It can't go on like this. Now Amir Khan is gone too. He had said: "It's in my will, they all

---

6. Ghasem and Ali Akbar Hossein are two of the central figures in Shi'ite elegies. They symbolize the martyrdom of innocent young men at the hands of the infidels in the battle of Karbala, itself the ultimate symbol for the Shi'ite cult of martyrdom. See also note 22.

know. If I have an attack, I don't want my carcass to lie around in a corner or be thrown on some hospital bed."

After Ashkan, he wrote his will. He brought and showed it. No, maybe he wrote it after his wife, Hajie Khanoum, died of grief over Ashkan's death. He had taken the title of *The Demonic Decade* from his will, or from a conversation. He used to say: "I know I'll die in this demonic decade. The sooner the better."

And this, coming from him, who had seen and suffered so much. It hadn't been easy, from 1941 to the present.

He would say: "Believe me, there were at least one hundred thousand people in the May Day demonstrations of 1953. That was no small number. What do you think Tehran's population was? It wasn't even a million. I'm sure it wasn't. Then, later, on the nineteenth of August when the likes of *Shaban the Brainless* poured into the streets, not a single one of that crowd showed up. Of course, we had our orders. How much do you think they tortured Vartan, a simple party member?[7] When they found him in the desert beyond the city, he was badly mutilated. There were cigarette marks all over his body."

"Then . . . Just forget it. I don't want any part of this anymore."

He wore a black shirt. To smoke less, he had a cigarette roller. He rolled them every morning. He wished he had asked him when he began wearing a black shirt. Now Pari and her husband and Amir Khan's sons were all wearing black. He

---

7. Vartan paid with his life for membership in the Tudeh Party. He has often been eulogized, in prose and poetry, as one of the symbols of resistance in those years.

would buy one, for sure.

Of death he didn't want to write, or of the *Hejlebs*, or of the cemetery for the infidels on Khorasan Road where even headstones are not permitted. And occasionally a bulldozer is brought in to raze the graves. In the last few days he had been constantly thinking of the statue of the angel, made of plaster, standing in the little pond in the middle of the garden, a swan held aloft on two hands. It was white and from the gaping mouth of the swan, water gushed out and washed the angel, and the swan too. The angel stood on one leg. One of its wings was cracked. If he were to write about it, he would have one of the wings broken. But in fact, he hadn't allowed it to break. Even this year, in the month of January, he had wrapped it with a sack, then covered it with plastic, and tied it all with a rope to the sawtoothed edge of the little pond. Around March, he would unwrap it and wash it clean. The foot that stood on the ground would be covered with sludge; probably from the water that sifted through and gathered in the little pond. The foot that hung in the air would remain white. Of course, not so white as not to need washing. He washed it as he washed his daughters in their infancy, with soap and a washcloth, from toes to thighs, and the two thin loins and the little protruding belly, white like infants'. It even had a navel, and two little round white breasts. His daughters would probably laugh again. This time, he would have to spend one of his mornings on her. In exactly two months and a few days. And when they would return, they would see it white and clean, standing on one foot, water dripping from the short plaster hair, or from the curve at the end of the elbow. Then, at Zohre's clap, he would turn on the fountain.

Why couldn't he write of these? Were not these his favorite little consolations? If he were to write for himself, this is what he would write about, and not about what he had written for those who had fled abroad, or those remaining here who enjoy only cryptic allusions. It's like pouring salt on their open wounds, or like moaning and groaning to themselves.

For Amir Khan, the demonic decade was the eighties. And it began with the death of Ashkan, or the death of his wife. What about him? In what year did it begin? His heart might suddenly stop beating, or an artery in his head might simply burst. The first thing Amir Khan had said was, "Son, my head."

His daughter-in-law heard him. He, pale-faced and wide-eyed, was pressing his temples. That was it. Somewhere in his head, one of his arteries could not bear it anymore. And all the time he had been thinking: "Why wasn't it me?"

He would say it at any funeral he went to. It was nothing unusual, he would just put on a jacket, grab an overcoat, and off he went.

His decade may indeed be these years. This time someone was ringing the bell and didn't want to lift his hand. He looked; it was still blank, a whole pile of blank papers.

Let them ring.

And there was also the pomegranate tree, his consolation of late April that would last well into fall, and sometimes even early winter, especially when it blossoms and looks like bonfires lit atop a green mountain, and one could stand afar and imagine a group of people sitting around each one of the fires, just like those years when they would circle around fires here and there in the mountains, and then only they—with eyes burning from the smoke, and from having blown into the fire—would sing "Kiss Me"[8] in a baritone voice. Two of them escaped with their families, and one of them was there in his old age. As Naderi would say, his old syphilis had recurred.

No, it won't work like this, when everything rushes on simultaneously. How much room is there on a page, or even on several pages? He had to stop somewhere, like a man placed in a cell with only one window. Then, one could see the whole world through this one opening, or rather, through this grated or barred window.

He got up; he could think about it on the way. He only put on his overcoat, shopping bag in hand, feet in slippers, he took his wife's note from the clip on top of the rice-cooker. On the way, he would read the list and then do the shopping.

The little store wasn't busy. The *Hejleh* was there on the street corner; the ones clad in black numbering four or five. There was no sign of alms dates. He stopped and looked at the picture. How easily they go, even over mine fields, free of attachments, as if they fly. Yet, it was in him that the roots had deeply run reaching all the way back to Tous or even Nizami's Ganja, through every line of *The Seven Beauties*.[9] He

---

8. The reference is to the years before the Islamic Revolution, when young radicals, full of optimism, went mountain-climbing and once away from the gaze of the secret police, occasionally sang a song called "Kiss Me." A myth in its own right, the song is often thought to have been composed by a political prisoner the night before his execution; it symbolizes resistance and optimism in the struggle against oppression.

9. Tous is a city in Iran where Ferdowsi (932-1025 or 26), the greatest epic poet of Iranian literature, was born.

Nizami (1141-1203) is an epic poet; his five great works have been assembled in a

used to teach *The Black Dome* every year, even toward the end of the decade. Everyone wears black. A city, or maybe the world. In the beginning, there is only a wanderer who is the guest of the king. Then, little by little, every fiber of the king's soul is pulled to the city, engulfing it, as he seeks the key to the riddle. He sets out. When he arrives, he finds the entire city clad in black. So everyone knows. Yet no one speaks. He befriends a noble butcher. Well, that was the story. That is what he read. What counts is the interpretation. It has to be an inner experience, everyone must go through it. Surely for Nizami it meant never reaching Utopia, never reaching that which is beyond the seventh heaven. No room for the angel, the moon, or the sun, for all that is beautiful is but a material incarnation of its light.

That you may know why all who silence keep
are in this manner dressed in black attire.[10]

So he sits in a basket, and with the power of magic reaches the top of a tower. The rest is clear. Similar scenes abound in other stories. Scenes about how, with the help of a bird, they travel to a distant land, to a Utopia that never existed, even to a dream.

He stopped in front of the vegetable stand, last in line. Which one of them had experienced it? He wasn't joking.

---

collection called *Khamsa* (The Quintet). The greatest of the five is *Seven Beauties*, comprising five thousand verses and composed in 1197.

Ganja is a city that during Nizami's time was a part of Iran and is now in the Soviet Union and called Elizavetpol.

10. All the verses from Nizami are from: Nizami. *Haft Peikar* (Seven Beauties). Tr. by C.E. Wilson. 1924. London. 116, 122, 126, 127, 128, 130, 131, 132.

Leaving aside the women, for example the ones with the black chadors[11] who are eternally ebony-clad, or the ones wearing long tunics, with scarves on their heads. One man could be considered benighted. His suit was black, but he was still wearing a sweater, blue. He was in the middle of his demonic decade. Every day, there would be news of someone's death, a relative or a friend. After sixty, it is better to not even bother taking off the black. Suddenly, the woman in front of him was fixing her scarf. She tucked the blonde colored tuft of hair under her scarf. Then she told the women in front of her. She let them know with a poke of her hand. He understood. It was a patrol car. The Toyota had now stopped.[12]

That's how it always gets ruined. Past and present are no different. Otherwise, what is there in common between so many "panegyrics of the prophet,"[13] "praise and acclamation for the king," or even for the Ascension, and the king who sets out to discover why the wanderer wore black. Nevertheless, I have to buy one. They are dying, one a day, even some of his students, like Sadeghi who had a heart attack at age thirty-two. He would go and buy a ready-made black suit. It's not right. In the afternoon, completely clad in black, he would go to the mosque. He had seen how some could never take off the black. No, that is not what Nizami meant, though

---

11. Chador is part of a traditional Moslem woman's attire. It covers the whole of the woman's body, with only her face visible to an observer.

12. Islamic patrols that roam the cities of Iran in search of political or spiritual deviants drive around in Toyota Station Wagons.

13. The reference is to the fact that most Iranian poems, including Nizami's *Seven Beauties*, begin with praise for the Lord, the Prophet, and the King, only to continue in realms unrelated, if not in fact contradictory to such panegyrics.

he did compose the poem late in life. The seven domes that parallel the seven heavens, and the point of good fortune that rises from the center of one and connects to the other. Where are they taking me? When his turn came, he also bought some fruit. Where was the shopping list? He remembered. If he could only arrange these colors, or describe the contours that frame the colors, or the ragged rim of the sweet basil leaf, he would have paid due homage to this era. Then he started walking. In those days, he would even write on paper money. He had to stop in the bookstore. Occasionally, he went there. He knew he wouldn't buy anything, but at least he could touch the books. At times, he even sensed them. The Toyota was there. He saw them again, the same four people. What could they want with him when it had been years since he had published anything? He had seen his own books on the inspector's desk in the Ministry of Guidance, stacked one on top of the other. Two of them he didn't even have himself. He hadn't been blacklisted, yet he had to amend a line here, and correct another one there. No, he was past the stage of making these changes, particularly to lines that had effervesced from some deep, unknown layers of the land beneath this spring. Now all of them, good or bad, stood stacked on the inspector's desk. How nice if they had just given him that collection. They even had *The Demonic Decade*. He had seen its spine. It had a pleasant green color.

No, he must think of those colors, or better yet of the falling snow. What day of the month was it? The fourth of January 1982, exactly half-past ten in the morning. He had only one or one and half hours left before his daughters would return.

In the bookstore, he would glance rapidly at the titles of the books on the shelf. Two new ones were out. He didn't know them. The clerk had come to know him by then. He leafed through one of the books. Another chronicle of momentous moments, as if nothing significant had ever happened before. They all preface their books with a line from Hafez,[14] and then nothing. They too were living now, but not as part of the chain that links one to the other, and through him goes on to eternity. It's never as simple as they make it out. It isn't at all clear where that angel comes from, but it probably isn't much different than this. And then, all it needs is patience and forbearance, lest one open one's eyes and find himself again in the basket. For now it had left him. He had strayed too far and had been capricious, and it had left him because he had spent the most intimate hours not with it, but with a surrogate.

There was some snow, but it would melt. It sat on dry branches or occasionally on a leaf. He wished for snow, the trouble of clearing it notwithstanding. The girls would give a hand. It would even settle on his head. His hair was not white yet, only flecks around his temples and mixed in with the straight hair at the front. He still had time, another opportunity to come leaping, the way Nizami had described. Once home, he would again read the passage where the king arrives at the fated place and lets go of the bird's feet. Well, it's obvious: It's a place not here, nor anywhere that has ever been, or that will ever be. He wanders around until dusk. He thought he saw

---

14. Hafez is one of the greatest lyrical poets in Iranian literature. He was born in 1325 or 1326 and died in 1390 or 1391. He is the master of the Ghazal, a Persian poetic form similar to the sonnet.

the Toyota following him. He quickened his pace. He wanted to read the passage in which the wind blows all the dust away, and clouds appear and lay a touch of moisture on everything. Then, the fairies come, leaping, candles in hand, they lay out a carpet and set up the throne, and then, in keeping with their rituals of feasting, first the harp, and then the cup bearer, and that cup with seven lines on it.[15] If he had been present, he would say, as Khaghani had said, "Pour me a thimbleful more than the others." Small recompense for a line here and a word there he had written. And then comes the Fairy Queen, who ascends her throne. No, he didn't want these lines. He craved the part in which the fairy comes leaping—not for him, but for the King of the Benighted, the king who then wore black, all his life—and beckons him to the feast. He had read it often. He had even memorized it, and now if he could recall the first word of every line, he could recite the entire poem.

Once back, before he could put away his purchases and get himself to the basement—how nice it would have been if he hadn't covered the angel and could see it once whiten without him having worked hard for it—they were knocking at the door. Let them wait, whoever they are. While opening the book and finding the passage, he heard noises from the yard, like things were crumbling. He only had time to read up to where the queen says:

---

15. Seven is a particularly significant number in Iranian culture, mythology, and religions. The seven lines on the cup correspond to the medieval cosmic notions of the seven heavens; once again a microcosm is the metaphor for the macro-cosmic order.

Khaghani is a famous Iranian poet (1106-1185) imprisoned for a while and notorious for the difficulty and obscurity of his verse.

> *. . . It seems to me someone is here,*
> *an earthborn one who has no right to come.*
> *Rise and go around the circuit (of this place)*
> *(and) bring before me whomsoever you see,*

that he saw, and understood. For a while he had to bid farewell to all things of this nature. Or maybe, in fact, it was his turn. By now he knew their manner of conversing, their style of greeting, their ostensible apologies. That's why he thought that this lineage, if there is in fact a lineage, comes from the beginning of time, or from Beshar-ibn Taharestani, the poet known as "The Chained," meaning the slave, whom Mehdi, the Abbassid Caliph, The Guide of The Pious, accused of heresy, and after having him flogged, ordered his body thrown into the swamps of Bataeh, to Ferdowsi, who was not buried in the Moslem cemetery, to him, and then to eternity.[16] If indeed what happened in those dungeons to people like Kaab-ibn Ashraf[17] must also happen to him, then it would have to begin like this. Suddenly they arrive, unannounced. And he sat waiting so that he too could get his share, or, pay his dues.

They said, one of them, "Why didn't you open the door?"

"Does it make any difference?"

"Don't you even answer the phone?"

---

16. Beshar-ibn Taharestani was an Iranian poet born in 783. Many of his poems were tributes to Iran's pre-Islamic grandeur and denigration of the Arabs.

Mehdi was the third Caliph of the Abassid dynasty (749-1258); he ruled from 775 to 785.

Bataeh was a city near Basrah (Iraq).

17. Kaab-ibn Ashraf was a man of Jewish origins and an opponent of Mohammad, the prophet of Islam.

"I already told you."

He leafed through the book to at least find out how it happened, how the king, not yet clad in black, was taken near the throne. He knew there would be no similarity. Never. It's different every time.

Another person, waiting outside, was opening the gate, as if they wanted to come in with the car. So, in this decade, they take you away in cars, in Toyotas, made in Japan. What is Simurg[18] a metaphor of in China? Is it the sky? No. Is it eternity, piety, and sometimes even the pious man himself? That is why the king goes to China. In miniatures, it looks like he is made of clouds, or comes from the heart of a cloud, with open wings, wreathed with long, thin feathers of different colors, each a different shade, as if he had a colorful cloud for a crown, and it would sway here and there, turning upon its own back and neck, all the way to its tail.

One of them asked again, "What are you reading these days?"

He showed him the pleasant green color of *The Seven Beauties*.

The same man asked, "You too play tricks?"

"What tricks?"

"You know what I mean."

He picked up the book, laughed, and said, "You can see, can't you?"

He leafed through the book, supposedly to read the same passage. But it was for his own sake. The man snatched away the book. He turned a few pages and then opened the book

---

18. *Simurg* is a central metaphor in Iranian literature. It embodies the idea of wisdom and prudence and lives atop a mythical mountain.

where his pencil was. He placed the book on the table. Yes, they were indeed taking all his books off the shelves. They had brought cardboard boxes and ropes as well. They had closed the gate. The Toyota was now probably in the yard. He looked at the plastic cover of the angel and the branches of the pomegranate tree. He would remember.

"Get up," he said.

The good thing was that he already had his clothes on. He took his pack of cigarettes and matches. Nowadays he smoked less, only a few each day. He was near the end of his decade. One of them was also holding a burlap sack. He said, "Please don't put them in a sack, they'll be ruined."

"Just get up."

The man jerked him off his seat. How had he grabbed him? He smiled again. But he knew this would not be like other times. The sack was for his head. Not the lint that sneaked into his nose and nostrils, nor the smell of the rice; what bothered him was the way they were tying him. They were wrapping the upper half of his body in rope. No place to laugh now. When the girls return home at twelve, they'll know from the empty shelves. His wife was by now accustomed to it. This was the third time. By the orders of the Caliph, Beshar too was surely put in a sack. Kaab, at the instigation of one Brother[19] from the tribe, was thrown into the thorny, poisoned bushes of Gazian. How many years did Masoud Saad Salman spend in the dungeons of Nay, Dehak, and Lahore?[20] He

---

19. The French Revolution brought us the concept of "citizen." The October Revolution inaugurated the notion of "Comrade." The Islamic Revolution has given us "Brother" and "Sister."

must go. He was paying his dues. What were the first words of those lines by Nizami where the King of the Benighted took to the air? They also tied rope around his feet, and one of them said, "Get moving."

Surely they were joking. He had no choice but to hobble along. His head bumped something, and his hand struck a cardboard box. He heard them filling the boxes. He tried to move at least to the doorway of his library. The rest would be their problem. Suddenly a blow came down. It was not a fist. They had nothing in their hands. He swayed back and forth, or maybe he had just wobbled a bit, about to fall, and someone had grabbed him in mid-air. Only with a book could they hit like that. But with which one? It didn't matter. So long as they hit with a book and on his head, then there is something to rejoice for. He even managed a smile, and again smelled the rice, and had to spit out the lint. They had lifted him from the waist. His ankle probably bumped into the door, and that helped soothe the whirling sensation. Then they grabbed his feet, carried and hurled him, stiff and straight, onto the metal floor of the Toyota station wagon; that was certain. They occupied the seats themselves. The backs of his hands hit against a cardboard box, surely full of books. How great if it ended right here, a happy ending, a blow to the head, right in the middle of his books. But how could all of his books fit in such a small place? Wouldn't it be better if they just put his

---

20. Masoud Saad Salman is a well-known Iranian poet (1046 or 1047 to 1121 or 1122), particularly famous for his "prison poems."

Nay, Dehak and Lahore are cities in the dungeons of which Massoud Saad served some time.

own books next to him? Or maybe they could bury him under all the copies of his book that remained unread in the bindery for the last two years? Then, that would be it. He tried to sleep, although his sedatives were in his pocket. Well, Farkhondeh would not give up. She would go from one Revolutionary Committee to the next. The other time, when he was young, Mother, a bag of whey in hand, grabbed one of the men and said, "Are you going to give him this bag, or do I have to dump it on your head?" Now she would laugh and say, "His collar flew right off."

"It was probably worn out," he had said.

The officer almost hit her. They delivered the whey. A couple of days earlier, sister had brought the eggplants and the guards actually sliced them and prepared a dish of eggplant and whey. Only the vodka was missing. During his interrogation, he was slapped twice on account of that eggplant and whey. Maybe it was the same officer. Mother didn't know who he was. She said he was well dressed. But these men were like him, supposedly of the masses, dressed in trench-coats. For this reason he had refused to wear his own overcoat for a long time, though its lining was fur, and it was warm and comfortable. They drove around different streets, so he wouldn't know where they were taking him. He knew. To do this with him, he who had taught *The Black Dome* for so many years, was in bad taste. He wished he could see how many *Hejlehs* were in these streets. Several months had passed since the beginning of this umpteenth Karbala[21] operation. It was probably eleven in the morning of Saturday, the fourth of January, 1982. They had turned on the car radio so he couldn't exactly hear what they were saying over the transmitter. No, they hadn't brought all of the books. Maybe they were requesting more cars from headquarters. Even several Toyotas would be too few. In 1973, they only returned his classical texts. What about now? A cardboard box had fallen on him.

"How are you, poet?" one asked.

The other time, in 1973, they had said, "Poet of the masses."

It was better now. All of this talk about the masses certainly didn't fit him now. He thought of a stream, never seen before, that seemed to flow with tall reeds on both sides, and only occasionally was its very presence, and quiet flow, detectable from its one or two small ripples on the surface. Then he imagined a meadow, not a prairie but a grassland, grazed by sheep only a few days ago, and now the small leaves of its greenery barely as tall as the tip of a finger. There were also trees, all cedar,[22] not so old that the thickness of the trunk would surpass the reach of several men, but as thick as only one man's reach, and tall, so tall that the gentle breeze at the top could be told by the occasional swaying of the treetops. Where was he? How nice if he could have seen the rest in his dream. But he hadn't. He woke, instead, to the clamor of the

---

21. During the war with Iraq, Karbala was the name given by the Islamic government of Iran to many of its offensive operations.

Karbala is the single most potent metaphor for martyrdom in Shi'ite history. In 680, Hossein, the third Imam and the quintessential Shi'ite martyr, along with some of his family and supporters, was killed by the army of Yazid, the then ruling Caliph. Every year Shi'ite Moslems mourn this death with rituals of flagellation and Passion plays. Such rituals are one of the reasons Shi'ism is called "the religion of lament."

22. Cedar is of particular importance in Iranian culture and history. It is the tree of Zarathustra. It has even been suggested that the paisley design, so prominent in Iranian carpets, fabrics, and artifacts, is none other than a cedar broken and ravaged by the onslaught of Moslem Arab hordes.

radio. It sounded like the speakers were next to his ears. From the white overalls, he guessed the man must be a doctor. No, this was not a hospital; it was his cell. He could tell by the cold, damp floor. Through his clenched teeth, they had poured something down his throat, leaving a bitter taste in his mouth. Somewhere, in the middle of his head, there was still a burning sensation. He had arrived. He tried to sit. As he opened his eyes, he saw a pair of glaring eyes staring at him. Somebody sat in the other corner on a blanket folded over four times, his knees tucked up to his chest. The doctor, or whoever he was, said something. He couldn't hear. The blare of the loudspeaker would not permit it.

The doctor, or whoever he was, shouted, "How do you feel now?"

"All right," he mumbled.

He sat up, leaning against the wall. A cigarette was placed between his lips. To see the color of the flame, he opened his eyes. In the darkness of the cell, it would look more beautiful. Instead, he saw a pair of black eyes, so he closed his, and then took only a few deep puffs, and he saw once again the slow blue-like flow of the stream in the reeds. Somewhere, someone was sprinkling the prairie, surely not to celebrate his arrival.

And, he thought, they had intentionally given him something to make him unconscious. Now he felt a splatter of water from the hands of the doctor, or whoever he was. He said, "Please, let me sleep."

Then, the force of something like the toe of a boot pierced his ribs and came back again, and a voice shot over the clamor of the radio said, "Quit acting like a ninny..."

The rest he knew without having to hear. When he was slapped, he just let go of the cigarette. He searched for it with his hand, and brought it up to his lips.

The two glaring eyes were still fixed upon him. What a tiny mouth he had. Instead of fuzzy down, he seemed to have only a thin line of bristle on his cheeks. Where had he seen him before, that the contours of his chin and the arch of his eyebrows looked so familiar? An empty bowl and spoon stood before his slippered feet, so it must be past noon. He hadn't heard the *Azan*.[23] Who was delivering the sermon today? He listened. How appropriate if he would preach on heaven. But what could he have in common with heavenly boys and girls made of milk and honey? Neither the Arabs, nor the Gaz, not even the Turks or the Mongols had been able to take away his cedars. And the stream of clear blue water, with its small ripples, kept flowing from somewhere more remote than the place where Nizami composed stories from the remnants of *Shahname-ye Abu Mansur or The Khodai Namek*.[24] And then it would flow to a distant place, not yet in existence, and there, someone would again make something of the little fragments that he had written or would write. That was the only thing. The doctor, the man in white, got up, muttered something, and left. Now, he was alone. Still, those two eyes that belonged not to a face, but to the apparition that hung in the corner, were looking at him. He made a gesture and moved his lips.

---

23. *Azan* is a call to prayer made three times a day (at sunrise, high noon, and at sunset) in many Moslem communities.

24. *Shahname-ye Abu Mansur* and *Khodai Namek* are both books belonging to the pre-Islamic culture of Iran and essentially consist of accounts of the deeds of great Persian kings. They are both thought to be a primary source for later Iranian epic poems.

He was pointing to the bowl of food, covered with a piece of bread, on it a spoon. He had to eat. It had gotten cold. It was something like a gruel. Yet he ate it. Then he reached into his pocket; they had only left his box of cigarettes. There were always several sharp pencils, a small notebook, and even a pen in his pocket. His key chain was also missing but his blindfold was there. He was still looking at him. He introduced himself, first and last name.

"I know."

"You know?"

"I've known a long time."

Then he said, "And I am Sarmad. Just plain Sarmad."

He wanted to ask, Have you read a poem of mine? But he was too shy. In those days, he would occasionally hear that a student was arrested because of a book or even a poem of his. In 1973, they first arrested one of his students, and then came for him.

"Got any matches?" he asked.

He made himself understood more through gestures than words. Suddenly, he heard a click, and then saw the hole which had come to frame a mouth, a cave in a cluster of hair. He was cursing, not at him, but at Sarmad. Then the door opened. He saw the boots, and then a kick in either the ankle or somewhere else he could not see.

"If I only see or hear it one more time, you'll see what I'll do to you."

Then turning to him, he said, "You better shut up too. Talking is forbidden in the cell. This is no hotel. You get it?"

No, he didn't hit him. He raised his head. Where had he

seen him before? He surely wasn't one of the ones who brought him here. Maybe they all look alike. When they want to call each other, how do they know who is who? Of course, uniforms can help. Some wear name tags over pockets of their uniforms. This one didn't. He said, "Sorry, Sir, I only wanted a match."

"Sorry, Brother!"

The man had said it from somewhere so deep in his throat that he thought he would certainly be hoarse afterward.

He said, "Sorry, Brother, I didn't know. Is it possible . . ." and he pulled half a cigarette out of his pocket.

With a knock of the hand, he threw the cigarette on the floor and stepped on it. "Get up. Who gave you permission to have cigarettes?"

He got up. He couldn't lean on the wall. It was like a stream of water, as cold as that which had frozen his back and as wide as the palm of a hand, was running deep into every fiber of the wall. From behind the door, or through the hole, someone said, "Leave him alone. We'll take care of him later."

He sat down. It wasn't important. Luckily he wasn't that hooked anymore. One must be ready. From the beginning of his decade, from those earlier years, he had thought so, yet, he hadn't been ready. Maybe he had thought so much of the others, of those who were tortured, that in retribution, he began the destruction of his own body. That's why he got in trouble. With deliberation, out of shame, he paid with words for those many sleepless nights. His poems were banned, but they came out illegally, passing from hand to hand. Then they came for him. When the interrogator read them aloud, he himself knew they weren't really poetry. They still aren't. Now, they had published a selection of the poetry of these years, named *The Demonic Decade*, which, in reality, was his own decade.

Had his decade now ended?

He heard, "I have some matches. If you have another cigarette, I'll light it for you, on the condition that I smoke first."

It was Sarmad, speaking with his head down. Even when he lifted his head, he didn't see his mouth, tiny as a dot, move a bit. He too must learn. He had learned Morse in 1973, but this time, or at least as long he had been there, he hadn't heard anyone tapping on the walls.

He took a cigarette from the box and handed it over. Sarmad pulled out half of the striking edge of a matchbox and showed him half a matchstick. "You see, we're experts," he said.

He had heard that they split matches and that all the prisoners in a cellblock, all forty or fifty, smoke one cigarette. Smokers are given cigarettes twice a day, one per person each time, only those of course whose interrogation is over and who await sentencing: ten to fifteen years, and more often execution, group after group. No. He was beyond the danger of execution. The one poet they had executed caused more headaches than they had bargained for.[25] That's why they allowed him to keep his pack of cigarettes and the "Brother" hadn't hit him the way he hit Sarmad.

---

25. The author seems to be referring to Said Soltan-pour, a well-known radical activist and poet who was imprisoned both under the old regime and in the Islamic Republic and was executed in 1981, apparently on the charge of membership in a clandestine armed guerilla group.

Sarmad was smoking.[26] He said, "I killed two Revolutionary Guards. I've been here a year and three days. That's what they say and I guess it's not a lie."

Again he puffed. "Why have they brought you here?"

He looked at him. How had he survived till now? Well, he did have down on his face. He was only eighteen or nineteen, but he looked intelligent. Somewhere on his face, he seemed to have a nervous tic. Suddenly he looked in his pockets, they had not returned his glasses, the ones he wore for reading.

The cigarette was almost half gone. He could tell by the way Sarmad measured it, using his index finger, he gauged the distance between the filter and where the smoke came out. "I've two more puffs left. You didn't answer," he said.

"The Demonic Decade."

"What?"

He explained.

Sarmad would hide the cigarette in the cup of his hand and puff from the tips of his clustered fingers, exhaling in the direction of the grated hatch over his head. It would curl, but not enough to be visible. Maybe snow has covered everything and Farkhondeh is probably going from one Revolutionary Committee to the next.

"Read one of them."

---

26. Sarmad (which literally means the Garden of Eden) was, by all indications, a member of an organization called People's Mujaheddin of Iran. They are a radical group, committed to an Islamic version of socialism. Before the revolution, they were a small organization engaged in urban guerrilla activities. After the revolution, they emerged as an organization with a large popular base. Around 1984, they began an armed struggle against the Islamic Republic of Iran. Thousands of their members have since been executed or jailed. Their leadership, as well as the greater part of their cadres, now live in exile.

"I can't remember."

He handed over the cigarette and said, "Look at me; when I wink, put it out."

It really tasted good. In 1973, in the confines of those four walls, the comrades started a rationing system. In the beginning, they let him smoke his twenty a day for a week, then they reduced it. They said it was costing the commune too much. The commune more or less operated on his money. The others didn't have visitors. He consented, particularly because in the days and nights spent on restoring a badly damaged body, they had shown him such compassion. But his work began from the second night. After drinking their tea, the five sat around, heads stooped over, quiet. There were only two to a cell, but during lunch and dinner hours, they were allowed to be in one place; at night, they would stay together until lights-out. He was sipping his tea. His cigarettes were not yet rationed. He was into his second cigarette when Jahangir said, "Read something, what are you waiting for?"

"What?" he asked.

"Poetry, of course."

He reached over and opened the door a little. It was cold. It was not snowing but he could see that the big pond in the small yard was frozen. Their ration of kerosene was only enough to warm up their food; then they would take the small heater to the yard and turn it off. The night before they had talked about this and that. They were still being questioned. Jahangir said he was arrested for carrying weapons in the mountains. He said it was a frameup. A tribal feud. Of the whole group, only one said his daily prayers and during the day also practiced calligraphy in the cell. What was his name?

So they were waiting for him. He began with a poem of Nima,[27] but he couldn't remember all of the lines. A few nights later, he had read "The Loose Woman." What a look Bahrami had given him! He had been unraveling a pair of socks into a ball of twine. He had raised his head and looked at him. He later heard that on the way from the place where he was arrested to the basement of The Committee,[28] his entire moustache was plucked, whisker by whisker. Again he began from the first line.

Now shut tight the door, for no more
have I fancy to meet a single soul

He remembered more or less what he had said. He had read and read. He had said, "Well, here, in the middle of the poem, I've forgotten a few lines." But he couldn't explain what he had said or what he was saying. He had sipped his tea, and recited the poems, stanza by stanza. When it was over, he had returned to his tea; perhaps he had also lit another cigarette. Bahrami said, "Well?"

He probably showed his bewilderment by the expression on his face, for Bahrami added: "Read some more!"

He pushed forth his cup. Bahrami abandoned the ball of

---

27. Nima (1895-1959) launched the modernist tradition in Iranian poetry, disengaging verse from the strict rules of meter and rhyme imposed upon it by traditional Iranian poetry.

28. The Committee refers to a frightening set of buildings in the heart of downtown Tehran. It was the headquarters for the Committee To Fight Terrorism, composed of different security, police, and intelligence departments under the Shah. The daunting basement was where torture chambers were located.

twine and the socks, unraveled to the ankle, and poured him, and him alone, more tea. He said, "Sorry, finish your tea first and then read poetry."

Wasn't this how the ritual had always been? First they would fill everyone's cup, up to a line, with that acrid drink and the cupbearer would make the rounds. Maybe the poet or the muse would get a thimbleful more, and then with every line recited by the poet or the muse, the cupbearer would make the rounds again, and every line would end with a rhyme, and then the cupbearer would again make the rounds, all the way to the muse or the poet who would again get a thimbleful more. What a mess he had gotten into. He had no choice but to put out his cigarette and finish his tea, bitter as it was, in a few gulps. He read something, again from Nima. No, that was not what they wanted. Jahangir said so. Finally it ended in a discussion, with the same customary proclamations about art as a reflection of reality and the poet's indebtedness to the masses. He thought, Why have they brought me here? He had to go, they had to throw him out. But how could one associate with the likes of Siyahatgar or Naderi? It was more or less the same now. He didn't want it. He was fed up with this two-sided coin. He was not a poet of this era. But who has ever been? Maybe he could somehow get along with Sarmad. "How old are you?" he asked.

"Speak quietly," he heard.

With closed lips he couldn't yet. He heard, "I am nineteen, or maybe eighteen, but why should I lie? I am one thousand nineteen years and three days."

In other words, in the last year, he had aged a millennium,

or as they say, "for every millennium a minutia of growth." This little boy was that minutia of growth, still squatting in threadbare blue striped shirt and jacket, the right shoulder patched, with his head shaven, and so unevenly too.

He was about to put out the cigarette when he heard, "Give it to me."

He didn't look to see how far the cigarette butt was smoked. Head cast down, he asked, "What about the toilet?"

"They come around themselves, mornings, noons, and evenings, only. We've gone for our noon turn. But you can tell them you want to do your ablution."

"I don't say my daily prayers."

"You don't?"

He pulled the cigarette away from his curled lips. What a glitter in his eyes. In a poem, he should use a forged blade as a simile for those eyes. The butt that had reached the filter still gave out smoke. "Leftist?"

"What do you mean?"

"I asked whether you believe in God?"

"What kind of a question is that?"

"I just asked whether you believe in God or not. Just say yes or no."

There was an element of hatred in that low, monotonous, and atonal voice, shown primarily by the unnecessary pauses between words.

"Look . . ."

"Don't give me that 'look' business, just answer me."

Now he was looking at him. The hole was opened. "Are you going to shut up or not?"

It was somebody new, addressing someone down the corridor, "Brother, these two are constantly talking."

Again, he heard, "Don't be afraid, tell me, I have to know."

Was it Bayazid or Rabee[29] who had said unto Mohammad that the love of The One has so entranced me that I can no longer think of you or anyone else. He did not claim that these words, these lines whose length and rhythm, even their metric composition he commanded had so totally engrossed him that he could no longer think of anyone else. Yet the angel who occasionally appeared in a word or in a line, had indeed left no room for anything else.

With a key, perhaps, they tapped on the door. "Put on your blindfolds."

He saw Sarmad stand up, and, facing the wall, put on his blindfold. His was a double-folded cloth with an elastic band. Sarmad's blindfold was black. He put his on while still sitting down; he could only see in front of his feet. From the boots he knew there were two of them. The third came later. He was wearing shoes and regular pants. Facing the wall, Sarmad said hello. How well they can kick right on the ankle. It was not with a shoe tip. He convulsed in pain.

"Get up!"

Clinging to the wall, or maybe to the ground, or maybe to something or someone else, he stood up; one of them said, "Bring this one! And you, sit down."

He knew they were taking him for interrogation. But it was

---

29. Bayazid (d.875) is one of the greatest figures in Islamic mysticism.

　Rabee (d.801) is one of the few women in the history of Islamic mysticism to have attained a spiritual status equal to that of the most revered men of that tradition.

different from what he had imagined. Passing through the halls, he stepped on people, some squatting, others lying down. Occasionally, he heard someone moan, and the guard who was leading him occasionally jerked his hand or foot, throwing him off balance. Once, he even fell, and two hands, belonging to someone probably lying on the floor, held him. He was also not familiar with their style of interrogation. In what book of catechism were these guidelines set out that he had never seen? While writing, he was forced to sit with his back to the interrogator, and once, when on the pretext of asking a question, he turned around, he saw only a pair of piercing eyes through two holes of the sack covering the interrogator's face, and all the talking had come through another hole, where the mouth was supposed to be. He wore a robe. He was sure of it. That was when orders for flogging were issued. The excuse was that he had lied when he had written that *The Demonic Decade* meant nothing more than a decade of his own life. He didn't count. They were flogging him right there, near that endless corridor, seething with people, sleeping, half-sleeping, or sitting and occasionally moaning. They flogged his back, sitting down. He couldn't see who was hitting and who was counting. But did it matter? It was the same hand that had ordered the books burned and the same mouth that ordained the slaughter of all the men of the Guraizeh tribe,[30] and enslaved their wives and children. The first two or three blows were enough to bring him to shrieks. It was more than he could bear. From

---

30. Guraizeh was the name of a Jewish tribe at the time of Mohammad. They lived near Medina, the prophet's seat of power. Mohammad was himself present in the war of the Moslem community against this tribe.

under the blindfold, he could see a man, wearing striped underpants, holding a Qur'an in his hand. He said, "The recompense for every blow is more than daily prayers or fasting." Back then, in 1973, or even 1962, they held his mouth. Now he was free to shriek to his heart's desire. Obviously, those silencer-hoods that reverberated sound back to one's ears, and even nostrils, were now of no use to them. The man used something like a leather strap, and hit hard; not in the manner prescribed, that is, flogging while holding a book under the elbow without it ever falling. Maybe he couldn't keep up with the counting because he had passed out. When again he saw the hem of the striped underpants, he was once more seated with his back to the interrogator, pen in hand.

He heard, "On your way back, remember, fix your blindfold. Did you get it?"

Yes, this he had heard in every millennium.

Again, it was a new sheet of paper, with this first question:

Q. What is your religion?

He turned around to ask, haven't you claimed that inquiry into opinions is forbidden, and he had duly received his response: every act is legitimate if it helps safeguard the interests of Islam. He knew. He had read *The Rule of The Juriscouncil* [31] in the early sixties, but he hadn't taken it seriously. He wrote:

A. I am a poet.

And then, he put down the pen. He had to confront the

---

31. *The Rule of the Juriscouncil* or *The Islamic Government* is a book consisting of several of Ayatollah Khomeini's lectures on the topic of Islamic rule. It is widely thought to be the most important theoretical articulation of the Islamic Republic's claim to power and legitimacy. The book has been translated into English.

thread of agony, whose roots lay in the inner depths of that which might be called the Utopia of the body, and then, at one end, reached the far corners of the now derelict Samarqand[32] and at the other, ended in Utopia. He, too, had a pedigree, strain after strain, generation after generation, and though there was only one thread, yet, occasionally it appeared like a rope, interlaced by two strings, each in a different color, woven into one.

On his way back, blindfolded, steering through feet, and occasionally stepping on a limb, he decided to give Sarmad the same answer. But when they opened the blindfold, he realized they were now four; all sitting like Sarmad, two in the upper corner, one across from the place that had seemingly become his niche. This one helped him sit down. To have the pain traverse only the cycle of his own body, or maybe hoping to stifle the pain, he sat with his knees tucked under his body. It was the one sitting across who said, "It'll get worse if it dries out. Try to move around. Also, rub it with your hands."

Sarmad said, "For God's sake let's not talk. What they did to this old man was just because of talking."

He swayed back and forth. He could not touch it. So, there is no poetry reading here. It's not going to be like the other time, when they forced him to tell them one or occasionally several stories every night, and all with a ration of only three cigarettes a day. Bahrami would even give his analysis, and they all began the same way: "Of course, I'm not an expert in

---

32. Samarqand is an old city of Iran, now in the Soviet Union. It was the birthplace of Rudaki, the first great poet of the Persian language.

this area, but don't you think a poem or a story should . . ."

Finally, one night he said, "I can't concentrate without sipping my tea and maybe taking a couple of puffs on a cigarette."

They added one to his ration, and in the afternoon they even allowed him to walk alone around the little square garden in the yard. It had become part of their routine. He would walk and walk and think about who and what he should talk about, and then he would jot down notes, often only a few words, to remember the outline. The others were each in a separate place. Islami, and we could presume he was indeed a believer, would practice calligraphy and read *Nahj-al Balagha*.[33] Bahrami would jump rope, and Jahangir would also find something to occupy himself with. Occasionally he would wash his clothes, and someone else whose turn had come would stay in the cell to read the hidden book. He never did find out where in the cell they hid the book when the guards came for the weekly inspection. They had also assigned him a time for reading.

Again he stooped over. One of them said, "Did they hit hard?"

And then he gave his name, but it didn't stick in his mind.

"We had talked," Sarmad said.

And again, another talked, and thus, he came to know them all. While eating or waiting in line for the bathroom, and occasionally during ablutions, he found out what each of them had

---

33. *Nahj-al Balagha* is the collection of sermons and letters of Ali, cousin and son-in-law of Mohammad, the prophet of Islam. He is much revered in Shi'ite religion as the first of the twelve Imams. He was a Caliph from 656 to 661. He was assassinated by a political foe.

done. Why did they tell him?, "I haven't turned anybody in, I won't. They say if you sign the letter of repentance, we'll let you go. But they lie. Then they say, if you've really repented, give us the names. Later, they even . . . you know, some have become just like interrogators. The guy was my comrade; now, he is questioning me."

Or again . . . how much more was there? How much is there? At night, he might have been the one who gave him a needle and said, "With this, you can write your poems on anything you get your hands on."

"I have no papers."

"You'll find some . . . what about the cigarette box?"

Three of them were lying on their sides. One was standing or squatting, waiting his turn to sleep. Sarmad said, "For God's sake don't talk."

When his turn came to squat by their side, one of them said, "Can you remember a poem or something?"

"Please, forget it and go to sleep," he said.

"Tomorrow, or the day after tomorrow I'll be executed. The sentence has already been handed down."

With his head bent over his knees, he read from the oldest poem that had been written in this language.

Merrily live with the ebony-eyed beauties, merrily,
*   for the world is no more than a tale and a wind.*
Saddened about the present we must not be,
*   recollections of the past we must not have.*

And he read up to this line:

alas, the world is a mere wind and a cloud;
              Bring forth the wine, and carefree be[34]

"Let's go to sleep!" Sarmad roared.

Another said, "We sure didn't have the time for it."

He said, "You can substitute anything for the ebony-eyed beauty; your ebony-eyed beauty was your party or organization."

"What was yours?" Sarmad asked.

"I am a poet, that's all," he said.

And again, the first one, what was his name, said, "Read it again, please. What is it called?"

"*Ghazal*,"[35] he said.

"Read the same one."

He did.

Another said, "You mean, when they line us up in front of the firing squad, we can sing this?"

He sounded just like Bahrami. Bahrami would say, "These poets and writers only talk. I'm not talking about you. I myself first got involved in this thing through these works. And I don't regret what I've done, but I realized later that these are all means to reach our goal."

"What goal?" he had asked.

He had looked at him with surprise. Later, they gave him ten years, and he saw him again in February of 1978, probably

---

34. The poem is by Rudaki (b. 850-860 and died in 940).

35. Ghazal is a one-rhymed form of verse that is very popular in Iranian literature. "It consists of about five to fifteen distichs with a rhyme pattern, aa, ba, ca . . . It is the truest and most pleasing expression of lyricism, particularly of the erotic and mystical but also of the meditative and even of the panegyric." See: Rypka, Jan. *History of the Iranian Literature*. Dordrecht, 1956. 90, 91.

carrying a gun under his overcoat. He had said, "What do you say now? Your books are selling well."

Someone had published them with a blank cover,[36] and soon they had become preciously hard to find. He could read one of these, so that when blindfolded, or wide-eyed, they stand facing the Brothers they can scream . . . "No," he said, "You know, you have to make a choice."

Someone, it was surely Sarmad, said, "Choice?"

Another tapped him on his feet, the one who had given him a needle, and on the way back from the toilet, after his ablution, had thrust a square piece of paper, the size of a palm of a hand, into his pocket.

He only read the *ghazal* one more time, and said, "Go to sleep."

When his turn came, Sarmad got up and sat in his place and he, in his sleep could only see the endless meadow, filled with cedars, where the slow swaying of the distant treetops was the only indication of the blowing breeze. And he was nowhere. He even knew he did not exist. He woke up with a kick from one of the Brothers, "You don't say your prayers, but don't you even want to go to the toilet?"

Then, it was time for interrogation, and when he returned and removed his blindfold, no one was there, not even Sarmad. The sound of the evening *Azan* could be heard. Why hadn't he heard anything? Wasn't it rumored that they executed people right near the cellblocks? At times, right behind the walls?

---

36. On the eve of the revolution, many books banned by the old regime were printed in pirate editions. They all had white covers. Soon "Blank Cover" became a notion well understood by all literate Iranians.

Dinner was a piece of bread and a morsel of cheese. There were two servings. Tea was poured in their bowls. He had washed his earlier. These were their rituals. They would make them crave even a hot cup of tea. Wasn't that how they indentured free men? So, one person was returning. Surely, Sarmad. The three cigarettes were also his ration. When he asked about matches, they said, "Only one of the Brothers has them. We'll let him know when he comes back." He had lit his first cigarette during the interrogation. It was the same Haj Agha.[37] This time he wanted to know the meaning of the poems. There was also another poem, not one of his, and they wanted to know what, for example, "the broken cedar" and "a rampaged garden" were supposed to mean. This time he was sitting blindfolded, facing someone who surely had a sack on his face. From underneath his blindfold he could see two hands. The agate ring was on the little finger. The sleeves were surely those of a robe. Why should they know? He had heard that some writers, and even poets go to Qom[38] to give them lessons. Where were they taking him? He whose Fairy Queen was now that plastered angel, wrapped in a sack, covered with plastic. He said, "If you don't cooperate, religious law commands us to flog you."

That day there was none of it. It was on the third day that

---

37. *Agha* means Sir in Persian. *Haj* is a shortened version of Haji, a much respected and coveted title bestowed upon all of those who make the pilgrimage to the city of Mecca (Saudi Arabia). These days in Iran, Haj Agha often refers to members of the clerical caste. A robe and an agate ring on the small finger are essential parts of the official costumes of this caste.

38. Qom is a city near Tehran. It has been a traditional center of Shi'ite teaching, and it is now the spiritual capital of the Islamic Republic.

he was flogged again. This time, lying on a bed, hands and feet tied to iron bars, with blows on the ankles and the soles of his feet. Sarmad forced him to lie down, and then walked on his muscles and massaged his feet, and even held his arms, so that he could walk around the cell or stamp his feet. He was happy to see Sarmad. He didn't know where the others were. He said, "Maybe they've been sent to one of the communal cells." Maybe the next day, another four or five people joined them. Sarmad had already told them who he was. Two were brothers; not twins, but alike. Suddenly, they jumped up, he didn't understand why, and embraced each other. They wept and quietly murmured something. He only understood that they were apologizing to each other. One lay down, the other sat by him. Then, neither was willing to go to sleep. All night, in the two facing corners, they sat by the others. He heard:

"Did it hurt a lot?"

"Don't worry, Dada."

"Are you going to let us sleep or not?" Sarmad said.

He was talking loudly. They stayed for three nights. He again recited some poems, even told them a story from *Shahnameh*,[39] flavored occasionally with a recollected line of poetry. By then he could talk with his lips closed. Then he fell asleep still sitting. When he woke up he saw them still there, lying side by side, with blankets over their infected feet. At dusk they got up and pressed their ears against the wall. They were

---

39. *Shahnameh* is one of the greatest works of epic poetry in Iranian literature. It was composed by Ferdowsi and is considered the most comprehensive account of Iranian mythology.

counting. He too heard. It was just the way he had heard it would be, like a truck full of steel unloading its cargo. It was far away, and then they counted. They said, "Twenty-three people." Sarmad was not there. Occasionally, around dusk, they would take him away, and when he would return his face would be washed, at times he would be even wet all over.

By then he knew he had fallen into the morass of their rituals. One gave him his underwear and another gave him his sweatshirt and overcoat and somebody else his sweater. This last one had pointed to his shirt, "One can go with this too."

He would read for anyone who asked, from any poem he could remember, all before Sarmad returned to the cell. If he wasn't being interrogated, he would needle the first words of verses and lines on a piece of paper, and then would read them. Each time, it was Sarmad that was left for him, with his two black eyes, connecting arching eyebrows, the hint of a beard on his countenance and a cleft in his chin. Even during their outings for fresh air, once a week for only twenty minutes, he was right behind him. He wouldn't talk. He knew him by then. Which group was it, when he finally told the story of *The Black Dome*? Fall had come again. The spring, he hadn't even seen. He knew of its coming only from the weather, and the occasional scent of distant grass that filled the air. He turned the sweater he had received as a gift into a pillow. And then, apparently, fall came. And every few days, three or four and once even five new people would arrive. The last group, all from the same organization, had been badly beaten. They wouldn't talk. Two were wearing black shirts. When in the morning Sarmad called one of them by his name, "You"—he

knew his name—"can you give me your shirt?," he was re-
minded of *The Black Dome*. During dinner-time, when their
bowls were filled with water, a few beans, and something that
looked like a piece of meat, and they sat leaning against the
wall, he began the story. He had needled the first words of
some of the lines on a piece of paper, and even on the torn
corner of a newspaper. Once, someone had even brought him
a whole interrogation sheet. He said, "I don't care what's going
to happen. I know in a couple of days they'll take you all and
. . . But I want to tell you one of the stories from Nizami's *The
Seven Beauties*." And he read.

Once there was a fortunate and mighty king,
*   To sheep and wolves he had given security.*
He had seen troubles, but had bravely striven
*   and through injustice (suffered), dressed in black.*

And then he told them, in prose, of the wanderer, clad in
black, and the King of the Benighted who left his kingdom to
go to a city in China and see why the wanderer had worn
black. He then told them of the people of that land, all dressed
in black, from head to toe. Yet none would divulge the secret
to him. He told them up to the point where he befriends a
noble-hearted butcher, and he finally takes him to a ruin.
Once the king was in a basket, he read,

When my body took its place in it,
*   my basket, bird-like, rose into the air.*
By some ring-working magic mechanism,
*   to the ring-juggling sphere it drew me up.*

The king reaches the crest of a tower, and then, with the help of a bird, travels to the place where he too went in his dreams, specially in his constantly recurring dreams of the last few months. Then he talked of the coming of the fairies, candles and candelabra in hand.

When night (adorned) the world in different mode,
gathered collyrium up and crimson spurned.
A wind arose and swept away the dust,
A wind more gentle than the vernal breeze.
A cloud appeared like clouds of April-time
and o'er the verdure scattered lustrous pearls.
The road was swept and sprinkled by the shower
became with idols like a temple decked.

And he finally talked of the Fairy Queen, nay, the Sun, who ascended the throne, and then of their drinking rituals—of wine and verdure, confection and muses—and of the mystery of each line on the cup, all the way to the point at which the Sun-faced beauty beckons him to the throne. With stooped heads, they listened. Should he tell them of the kiss and the embrace, of clinging to the black snare-like hair, or of falling off the cliff into the cleft? When he read that the Sun-faced beauty said,

She said, tonight, with kisses be content,
no more scrape off the colors of the sky,

and offered him a Moon-like beauty to quell his burning passion, Sarmad suddenly erupted, "What kind of nonsense is this? We haven't come here for this kind of stuff." Even when the others showed their approval of the story, he would have none of it. He was shouting. And finally he got up and banged on the door, complaining to the Brother guard. He said, "We're young, we have many desires, we've never touched a girl's hand in our lives; and then this guy won't leave us alone with his erotic stories!"

He got a month, maybe more, in the dark cell. Sarmad hadn't told them what story he had been reciting. He was shouting, "I'll strangle him myself if he sleeps here tonight!"

The punches, the kicks, the curses were not important. What he didn't understand was why was it that of all people it was Sarmad who had complained? He had gone through this experience once before, ten or fifteen days in 1973. You only have to set yourself a schedule. After breakfast came walking, but around a figure eight, to avoid dizziness, and then, supposedly, a nap before lunch, and if the sun was out, he could watch the play of the sunbeams. He would take a long time with his lunch, and then again, walking, composing, anything. Several of the pieces he was now paying his dues for were the products of those very walks. He memorized them, and then when he returned to the communal cellblock others volunteered to learn them by heart. They weren't bad. Now he was forced to sit, from sunrise to sunset, and wait for the truck to unload its cargo somewhere nearby, after the *azan*; and then he could count the single shots. Occasionally he even heard the slogans they shouted. Apparently, girls were shot right near his cell. One evening he heard, "I only want to see my mom."

How old was she, anyway? Perhaps in this last year of his decade, in the place of the fairy, a brawling, fat-lipped demon would come to him. And that night, every night, demons danced around him, candles in hand, playing their cymbals, wearing those colorful short pleats.[40]

Why were they subjecting him to all of this? To eternalize this demonic reality through a poet? But how is that possible? Sarmad had squealed on his needle as well as his papers, so now he was left with a pair of sandals, that same sweater, and his own pants, which had now bagged around the knees. Even his jacket was not given to him. He had to count. To avoid nausea, he had to compose. Which letter did he have to sign? For what action must he repent? For which metaphor must he seek absolution? He would leave the walks for the afternoon, when the Brother guard did not care whether or not he in fact sat in his corner all by himself. In his prison, Masoud Saad Salman watched the stars from an opening in the dome, and learned astronomy under the tutelage of Bahrami. Occasionally, he even befriended an ugly pig-faced guard. What can one do with these? In the tenth or fifteenth day of solitary confinement in 1973, he began a game of fantasy, imagining spots on the walls and ceilings to be lanterns. After a day or two, the shredded corner of the rug began to look like a clown,

---

40. The reference here seems to be another poem in Nizami's *Seven Beauties*. It is the story of Mahan, a youthful man of leisure who sets out in search of worldly gains, only to reap a harvest of horrors. In one of these incidents, he sees the frightening sight of dancing demons, all fat-lipped and brawling. After many other horrifying adventures, he finds himself back in the house, with his friends all in mourning dresses.

and it would stick in his memory then, as it has since. Now, his companions for the nights were these apparent bursts of fire, and then something like single shots, and then what sounded like water gushing out under high pressure.

This time, the good thing was that after a few days the interrogation resumed, each day after breakfast. Now they wanted to know his whole life, from the beginning to this very moment, as he sat with his back to the interrogator, his blindfold lifted. Here there was no one in the hall. He had a blindfold. Yet the interrogator, another Haj Agha, had no sack on his head. He spoke with deliberation, as they often do, apparently trying to create his own particular style through special pauses and peculiar stresses. This one paused in the middle of the sentence, as if what was to come was of such significance that the listener should only hear it after prolonged concentration. Finally, it turned out he had had a visitor. A bundle of clothes had been brought for him. His name was written on it, in Farkhondeh's handwriting.

"Can I see her?" he asked.

"She's not here now; she brought them a long time ago." He glanced at the Brother Revolutionary Guard, standing at the door, and added, "Yes, it must be at least a month since she brought them in."

One could tell from the label, and he said, "But you . . ."

With the pause lasting for a long time, he interjected, "Excuse me, Haj Agha, but frankly . . ."

"Shut up!"

The words were said from behind him, and with them, shortly before or after, someone had kicked him, "You've no right to interrupt Haj Agha."

"As I was saying . . . " Haj Agha said.

The pause was here this time, but it had a sequel. Maybe it has always been like this. That is what he didn't want; this two-sidedness, this spiritual and physical hand that intermittently came down. All their poetry was exclusively limited to these two layers. Maybe Nima had realized this, and would no longer, at least most of the time, write two-layered poetry. And he, in every one of his poems since 1970, had only these two layers. And, most often, the overt layer was only an excuse. Where was that six-cornered diamond, or that chandelier with all those ornaments that he wanted to hang on this arched ornate ceiling. Where had he seen it? Haj Agha was saying, "You can talk to your family on the phone. Only tell them you're all right, just like it says here."

He slid a paper toward him. It was written in a staccato style: "I am well. It is a misunderstanding. God willing, it'll be over soon. How are the kids? I'll write. No need to come. Nothing serious."

Did it mean that something had happened abroad, or that one of these friendly or foreign radios had said something? New skin had grown over the scars on his feet. He had seen how occasionally someone's feet were patched with skin from his thighs. The boys called it "patch foot" and laughed, and then every night, the agonies of the patch, and of the dialysis of the kidneys would end with the unloading of the steel cargo; no, it would rhyme with the *Qur'anic* verses read over the radio, or better yet with the refrain in the *Al-Rahman* verse.[41] "Which one of the benefits of your Lord will ye twain count false?" That's the way it is. What business is it of others? He was more angry at them, those who count people here in terms of thousands or even millions, and then count themselves in numerals of one.

Haj Agha opened a folder and pulled out its scraps of paper. "But first tell me what does this needling mean."

He said, "They are the first words of verses by Nizami. His *Seven Beauties*. It might be among my books. They've brought them here." He couldn't bring himself to read all the lines that had rushed to his mind at the sight of the first words.

"They're not secret codes?"

"No, Haj Agha. Tell them to bring a copy of *The Seven Beauties*. I'll show you which lines each one of these words belongs to."

Almost snatching the paper away from him, he said, "Now, make your phone call. Just remember what I said."

He said exactly that. It was Farkhondeh. She wept the whole time, not even saying a word. Then he heard the voice of his Mahbanoo. She was preparing for her high school finals, or maybe the university entrance exam. Yet he knew they would not let her into the university. How could the Selection Center[42] at the Headquarters for the Cultural Revolution ignore her family name? She said, "Dad, we're all well. Take care of yourself."

His Zohreh was now about fourteen. When was her birth-

---

41. *Al-Rahman* is one of the most poetic pieces in Islam's holy book, *Qur'an*. The translation is from: *The Qur'an*. Tr. by T.E. Clark, Edinburgh. 1960. 544.

42. "Selection Center" is an Islamic euphemism for "ideological commissars." Their task is to purge all institutions, and in this particular case the university, of the regime's political opponents.

day? Which day in March? He said, "Is that you sweetheart? How are you? How many months till your birthday?"

The line was cut off, and a voice came on from somewhere and said, "No extra words."

Never was it connected again. Other sessions would deal with why he had not written any poetry since 1979. Not even about the war, with so many youngsters going to the front, longing for martyrdom.

He had seen their *Hejlebs*, and on television, he had seen all those people running, flags in hand, red bandanas over their foreheads, looking into the camera. Where do they put their *Hejlehs*? He knew, or maybe it was a rumor, that after every Karbala operation the price of a *Hejleh* increased, and he didn't even have a black shirt. He said, "I'm sorry, but I only see the war on television. Once I went to Ahwaz, even went as far as Sousanguerd, which we had only then recently recaptured."

For that he got in serious trouble. He was even flogged for having simply said Karbala. It was after Karbala Three, with the help of a cameraman from the T.V. station. He didn't say all of that, but simply added, "I went as far as Ahwaz; then, like everybody else, I went to Sousanguerd on a minibus. I stayed only one night. I wanted to see what was going on."

"Where is the poem then?"

Was he supposed to have written of those palm trees, now nothing but a dried trunk, lying on the ground, and even the trunk had been shot at from every angle. Or maybe he should have written of the man who was executed in Sousanguerd by mistake and of how they wanted to pay bloodmoney for him.

Once again, it was Sarmad who walked on his feet. Why had they brought him to his cell? He was wearing a black shirt, a pair of jeans, a sweater he had never seen before, and an overcoat. The overcoat stood hanging from the wall.

He said, "From today, they'll even bring us a newspaper." He pointed to them. He didn't look.

"I requested it for you. Usually they only give newspapers in the communal cellblocks. Just look at what we can make with them." He handed him a long tube. It was sturdy. "I want to put shelves here. I have seen it." The nail for his overcoat was also from a rolled piece of a paper.

"Don't worry. There'll be paper for you too."

He talked fearlessly, even loudly. He said, "I asked to come to your cell. I mean, the truth is that I got into a fight with someone on the communal block."

He pulled down the collar of his sweater. The mark of fingernail was visible.

"He wanted to strangle me. Only this cell had an empty spot. It's not fair that you should occupy this big a place all by yourself. And right next door, there are at least five people."

"And all sentenced to death?" he asked.

"No, they are still undergoing interrogation."

He was rolling a newspaper, with precision. He said, "What things they make from these newspapers . . ."

What did he want from him? He sat on his knees, facing him.

Now that he had heard Farkhondeh's sobs, Mah's requests, and even the suggestions of Zohreh, he felt stronger. To hell with the fairy or the demon. He asked, "Tell me the truth, why don't you leave me alone?"

"Me?"

"Stop working. Look at me," he said.

He looked. What a round face he had. Well, the down on his face formed a black aura around the sweetbrier of his cheeks and the forehead. The eyes were large, lips red and slender. His lower lip was quivering. The trepidation on his face came from the left side of his mouth.

He said, "You know, I don't say my daily prayers, so maybe I can't be touched with a wet hand, but you . . ."[43]

"I requested it myself."

"Do they care what we ask them?"

"Sometimes."

He waited for the quivering of the lower lip to subside. He even had a dimple. If they would allow his hair to grow long and waft, coils into coils, all hanging from the back, and if they had given this budding bristle to the blade of a barber, he would indeed be it. If Farrukhi were alive, many a poem he would write.[44]

"The truth is, I wanted to tell you something," he said.

"Leave it for later."

Sarmad pointed to the remaining pages of the newspaper. "Don't you want to read?"

Long before the ascent onto that tower, arisen to the moon, or this fall into the den, sunk into the purgatory, he would

---

43. According to Shi'ite belief, a person who does not say his daily prayers or is not known to be a Moslem is, by definition, "Impure" and hence cannot be touched by a Moslem. Should any bodily contact be made, ablution becomes necessary.

44. Farrukhi (d. 1037-8) is an old but still popular poet of Iran, known for his eulogies as well as his eloquent metaphors and similes. His deep appreciation and attachment to human beauty is rather famous.

not even glance at the headlines. It was probably about the war. It was the month of February. For him that was all that mattered.

Sarmad said, "You see, to the outside world, we don't even seem to exist."

"In these papers, yes," he said.

"No, before they used to give some news, not now."

Someone tapped twice on the door. "No talking!"

Sarmad said, "At least try to say your prayers."

"For these guys, or for God?"

"I used to do it for God, now I do it more for Haj Agha, who you haven't seen of course."

The second tube was also finished, and he was tightly tying the top and the bottom of the tube with a piece of string.

That was it. He didn't look at him anymore. He, too, didn't say anything. Next day, when he returned after dusk, Sarmad, walking on his flogged feet, said, "You see, it was no use."

"What?"

He didn't say. He tore a narrow strip from his worn-out shirt and tied it around the scar on his ankle. He said, "Yours has become threadbare." At night, he didn't say his prayers. He said, "I still have faith, but you know, there is one thing in Islam for which there is no repentance."

"What?" he said.

"You'll know later."

In the afternoon, he forced him to walk around a figure eight. He said, "You'll be set free. You haven't done anything. The worst you've done is to write a couple of poems. When your books won't come out, when they won't let anything of yours be published, effectively that means your execution. They know that."

"How? Where from?"

"You know I'm a repenter."

He had heard.

At night, as they lay side by side, Sarmad said, "I've read a lot. Of course, of your works I have read little. I was twelve or thirteen when my brother got me started. They executed him. He was the one who turned me in, yet he didn't repent. He wouldn't go for that, but we didn't become like those two brothers. You remember? They had hit each other. My brother was stubborn. He had to give a name, and he gave them mine, thinking I was only eighteen, they'll let me go. He didn't know. You remember, they issued a religious edict to execute people right in the streets. Every day they'd kill a few here and there. They hit hideouts with antitank weapons. Well, I couldn't. It didn't work out. For me, the end was when I saw the mutilated body of my brother. As they say, they only enlarged my feet by a few sizes a few times. That was enough for me. That's how it started. No, I didn't want to tell you all of this. I've come here only to hear the rest of that story. You do remember . . ."

"Then, why did you act like that the other night?" he said.

"I already told you."

"Told me what?"

He had turned around, and was now facing him. Under the dim light shining from the ceiling, his face looked blushed. No, it was the color of rubies, where it was outside the strip of dawn.

"You know, I even . . ."

He didn't say it. His eyes remained closed. Maybe he anticipated a knock on the door. How soon they had reached the end of their decade, and how he longed to reach the end of his. How easy it would be, and the sorrows of the quotidian, and, most important of all, the piercing pain of what, how, and why to write would no longer agonize him. The anguish of bread and rent, the chagrin from Zohreh, Mah, or even his wife could be hidden behind the mask of a poem. But what about he himself? How could he do justice to this era, and bear testimony to the nature of these decades and centuries, all before the end of March? For him, there was not much time left, and now, this one had come on his last night to . . . He should have strangled him. He turned his back to him and said, "I'm sleepy."

He shook his shoulders under the blanket. "Don't lie. One can't sleep with a sore back or a sore foot."

Still with his back to him, he said, "Leave me alone."

"Please tell me. I requested *The Seven Beauties*. They didn't have it. They say they've given all your books to the shredder. I could have had a visit with my mother. I didn't. I said, 'At least let me stay with him.' In return for all I've done for them, they accepted. They even accused me of you know what . . ."

He turned again. "Tell me, is tomorrow night my turn or yours, or maybe both?"

"You? Poor guy. You're going to survive. Don't worry. You'll have a heart attack, or maybe your blood will be so saturated with uric acid that you'll wish you were dead."

"So, it's your turn?"

"That's not clear either. What is clear is that they won't let me go. That I know. You know, I haven't left anything unsaid. I even turned in my fiancee. She was only fifteen. I mean, she turned fifteen when they executed her."

He said, "I wouldn't mind it either, but I have things, you know . . . My kids, my wife . . . So many unpublished and even unwritten poems. I don't want to fight these regimes anymore. Don't even want to bear testimony. Of course, that's exactly what I have done in that *Demonic Decade*. But now, I want to compensate. I've been cheated. For about ten years, my only audience has been people like you. Now, I realize I haven't written anything for a man in his forties, or even for myself."

And he thought, something that you would read and not end up wanting to aim and pull the trigger in your own mouth.

"You were saying . . ."

"I've told them, too. Maybe that's why they let me have you, or put me in that other damned cell. How many do they add up to?"

"Who?"

"The ones taken away at dusk."

"I didn't count. I wasn't responsible for them."

"Then let me sleep."

"I beg you."

He said, "You know that I don't remember the poems. And you are the one who blew the whistle on the piece of the paper with the first words of the lines. It is no fun without the text itself."

He said, "What does 'gathered collyrium up and crimson

spurned' mean?"

Out of spite he said, "Gathered collyrium is the darkness of the night, and the redness is that of the dust."

Then Sarmad began reading.

When night (adorned) the world in different mode,
*   gathered collyrium up and crimson spurned.*
A wind arose and swept away the dust
*   A wind more gentle than the vernal breeze.*
A cloud appeared, like clouds of April-time
*   and o'er the verdure scattered lustrous pearls.*
The road was swept and sprinkled by the shower
*   became with idols like a temple decked.*

He asked, "How was it?"

He said, "What a memory you have."

"With this memory, I've brought a lot of people in here. Worst of all was my fiancee. What did you call her? Sun-faced? They even confronted me with her. They had tied her to a bedframe. Hands to the bar on this side, and the mutilated feet to the bar on the other, in a way that she hung in the air. I had gone to tell her, 'It is no use.' She was unconscious. I loosened the rope around her hand, so that her stomach could reach the bed. She didn't open her eyes. She would only say, 'Water.' All of them want water. In that condition, water is poison. I myself drank water from an ewer in a toilet. I gave her water from an ewer, hoping she might regain consciousness. The more she drank, the more she wanted. Then she opened her eyes, but I guess she didn't recognize me. I went to her interrogator and told him that she might die. He didn't even send for a nurse. You know, we've had executions by flogging."

Then he said, "We were wrong. Can we understand the words of God better than Sheik Ansari, Naraghi, or Kulaini?[45] We were eclectics. I realized this . . . I accepted it. But that was not enough. I had to prove it."

"Why are you telling me all of this?"

"You tell me the rest of the story, and I'll stop. Then we can both go to sleep. I mean, you can sleep."

He said, "And then you'll go in the morning and report it all?"

"Report what? That you are a poet? That you want to live? That you want time to write poetry, to write the ones you haven't yet written, the ones no one has ever written, so that one day they'll name a street after you?"

He wouldn't stop. It was as if he had gone mad. He woke him even when he dozed off. "At least read a poem. A few lines after the servants took the King of the Benighted to the throne,

(Then) an attendant gently took my hand
and seating me upon the throne returned.

He said, "You're pulling my leg. You've read it."

---

45. Ansari, Naraghi, Kulaini are amongst the most influential scholars of orthodox Shi'ite theology. By calling his old political organization "eclectic," and by admitting the authority of these three clerics, Sarmad in fact repeats one of the main charges of the Islamic Republic against the Mujaheddin and their interpretation of Islam.

He said, "Believe me, I haven't. They just gave me your needled papers. I explained it to them. I read it for them word by word, and told them you had read up to here, and that the rest were only the first words of those lines of poetry."

"What else have you done?"

"Only if you are a repenter can you know the limits you might go to."

Then he rolled over and sat up. "You can complain to the Brother guard. That's usually the first step. That's why they are so strict with cigarettes and food rations, and even the toilet. You have to beg them for it."

He too sat up, with his back to the wall, and pulled the blanket over his feet.

"Do you have a cigarette?" Sarmad asked.

"Only one."

"How about smoking it together?"

He had the same patch of the striking edge of a matchbox with half a stick of a match. He asked about how a stick of match is split in two. He looked at the overhead hatch. Sunrise was still three or three and a half hours away. When he handed the cigarette to Sarmad to light, he didn't think he would let him go first. Yet Sarmad said, "You smoke first." Then he exhaled in the direction of the still dark hatch.

Oh, sacred morning with your white wand
Out of this prison of planks
Show them a new path
They, through torture,
Have become acquainted
With the most demonic of forces
yet they have resisted.
Their bodies are full of virtues and scars.

He laughed, and then asked, "Whose was this?"

"Paul Eluard."[46]

He then said, you shouldn't talk when it's your turn to smoke. It's my turn. You see, my body is only covered with scars, and old scars at that, one thousand, nineteen years, three months and three days old. Then, he said, all this time, that is, all through last year, particularly recently, sometimes every day, other times once every few days, around dusk, they had taken him to give the *coup de grace* for the sisters. He said, "I would stand in a corner, and when they mowed them to the ground, I would shoot them, one by one, in the head, I mean over the scarves, and then I would wash them with a hose, and carry them into the hearse, to be taken away. Every day was different; sometimes ten or twelve, occasionally even twenty. At times, there were only two or three a day. The problem was carrying them to the hearse. Well, I had an overcoat, I mean I still have it, and wear it outside. And then, I would wash off the blood, and stand near the heater to dry myself.

---

46. While the poem is indeed by Paul Eluard (1894-1952), the Persian translation used in the text departs in a couple of places from the French original. In the story, I have translated the poem exactly as it appears in the Persian version. The French original is as follows:

Saint Aube à la canne blanche
Fais-leur voir un chemin neuf
Hors de leur prison de planches

Ils sonts payeés pour connaitre
les pires forces du mal
Pourtant ils ont tenu bon
Ils sont cribles de vertus.

From: Eluard, Paul. *Oeuvres Complètes*. Vol. 1. Textes Etablis et Annotés Par Marcelle Dumas et Lucien Scheller. Gallimard. 1968. 1229.

But after all, it is a woman's body, and a young one's at that. I had faith, I still do. We made a mistake. We have to pay for it. I would give the *coup de grace* with dedication, and even care. But then, occasionally, even after all the water I had poured, and after washing off all the blood, the body would still be warm. Sometimes the scarves would slide off. Even if one side of the face had a big hole there is still something left of the lips and the cheeks. You understand, don't you? Even warm. The hair particularly was a problem. It would get wet, and then I couldn't tuck it under the scarves. The real problem was when the bullets hit one or two of the buttons on their dresses. It happened two or three times. The bullets leave a small hole through the chest; it's the back that is mutilated. At first, the pretext was to fix their appearance; then, I would just do a little too much of it. Well, it became a habit, and one day, when I lifted one to hurl on top of the others, what happened was what you said or were reciting."

He passed the cigarette. It hadn't passed the half point, but he gave it to Sarmad, hoping he would not say anymore, and asked, "What were the first words?"

Sarmad said, "Laid, harvest, pearl . . ."

He said, "I don't remember. Believe me."

He said, "Don't worry. They are not worried about you anymore. They know. I mean, I've told them. Suppose you want to say they are executing people. Well, go ahead and say it. What you only allude to they openly write in their newspapers. I've even heard that sometimes the Brothers, after having of course said the vows, and becoming grooms, go to the family of the girls and tell them that they had been their sons-in-law."

"What about you?"

"I told you already. I'll stay here forever. Or maybe, some-day, as I stand, hose in hand, washing the dead, they'll open fire on me. They sure don't want to leave any tracks. Just yesterday, one of them shouted, 'Hurry up, you bastard!' He was pointing his machine-gun at me. I told him she was still alive. Well, if he had fired, nobody would have questioned him. One day they will fire, I'm sure, because they know I have an incredible memory. Do you want to know the names of all those who came in that cell and were executed?"

He said, "It's in the newspapers."

He said, "No, they haven't been publishing that kind of stuff for a while. They only give the numbers. But it's not important, that's our law, it is in our tradition, our canon. One billion Moslems believe this. Or at least in words they do. So what can you do, or the ones like you, who shout their slogans behind this wall every day and then become corpses?"

The cigarette was nearing the filter. He no longer hid it in the cup of his hand. He took two puffs, one after another. "You'll be set free, I'm sure. But I . . . Maybe without yesterday's incident, I had a chance of becoming an office clerk for them. A small part in this gigantic machine. I would have even been happy."

"What happened yesterday?"

"Now you want to know?"

And he handed him the cigarette butt. "Here, smoke the rest. Maybe I'll ask the Brothers to give me a cigarette in these wee hours. You see, don't you?" He pointed to the window. Coryllium had gathered up. When had they turned the lights off?

He got up, went to the wall, stood there with his back to it, held his hands locked into one another, and said, "Go up. It's right across there."

"What?"

"Where I work. At nights, right here in the back, I ascend to the same place that Nizami's King of the Benighted went to."

"No." he said.

He sat right there, under the hatch. "You're afraid. You should be. Now even I am afraid. A couple of days ago, in the evening, I was standing farther back. Five girls were lined up, hands tied, eyes blindfolded. One was shouting slogans. She was as tall as my sun-faced beauty. Like every other time before, I thought, this must be her, and I thought, I can't give her the *coup de grace*. I didn't get any closer. The Brothers did their work. They stood around talking. I had only seen the tip of her braid. I recognized her from the curls at the tip of the hair. We were married by our organization, but I had never seen her without scarf. It was her all alright. It was different this time. I don't know, but maybe for at least a thousand times, I had imagined one of them to be her, and every time I had pulled the trigger. This time it really was she. She was the third person, curled up, and her hair was long, and had curls at the end, and was as you would say darker than black coal. I recognized her by the curls. She had covered her face. I couldn't give her the *coup de grace*. I only reached and pushed back her hair. It was she all alright. I fired once into the ground near her head and passed. When I reached the fourth girl, I looked back. She was looking at me. The Brothers had gone. The driver of the hearse was probably in the office. The sky outside is cloudy, you know. When I finished off the fifth girl, I went and put on my coat and plastic boots and washed them all with a hose. I thought she would be dead by then. I even carried her last. When I picked her up, she opened her eyes and looked at me, with that pale, pale color. Even her lips were colorless, with that wet hair hanging over her long black dress that clung to her body. When I placed her on top of the other four, I realized that her body was still warm. She was alive. She even moved her head, as if she didn't want to see or recognize me."

It was no wailing or weeping, but a perpetual sob that rose from the depths of a catacomb. Hoping to break this endless cycle of sobs, he said, "Will you go today too?"

"No. I asked them to give me another job. They refused. Again they talked of repentance and of the two Revolutionary Guards I had assassinated."

He stooped his head over his two knees, and from the depths of that labyrinthine catacomb, the moaning chain of sobs rolled, and out it poured, and kept on pouring.

The guards tapped on the door. "Time for prayers. Get ready."

They had to put on blindfolds and wait for the line to reach their door and then they would follow the line to the toilet.

Sarmad said, "They are going to let you go; I'm sure. Come on, put this on, it matches your hair."

He wasn't talking about his sweater. He took out his black shirt, "Hurry up."

Why did he wear it? Sarmad wore only his sweater and said,

"What do I need a shirt for?"

The cuff and the elbow of his own shirt were torn. He crumpled and threw it in a corner, and then put on his sweater and jacket.

Sarmad said, "Well, so long. But remember, you didn't read the rest. You did yourself a disfavor. As for yours truly, I'll hear it from Nizami himself in the other world."

He was laughing.

He didn't return that night. From afar, he heard the clamor of the unloading of the steel cargo, and nearby, only one steel bar fell. There was light in the window. Wedging his hands and feet against the wall, he climbed toward the window. Not even halfway up, they pulled him down. They didn't hit him. Haj Agha asked him, "What happened? What is wrong now?"

"I wanted to see the sun set."

"You'll see it, don't worry."

He didn't see. The sky was cloudy outside. Two days later, in the guard room, at the gate, they opened his blindfold and sealed his release papers. It was eleven o'clock in the morning of the fourth day of the month of January.

"Does my wife know?" he asked.

"Come and give her a call."

"No, it's all right."

He had no money. "Do I have to walk?" he asked.

They gave him his key chain, his watch, and glasses. The watch had stopped.

"You can go with the Brothers, but you know, you must again . . ."

They put on his blindfold, and again they aimlessly wandered around for a while, but this time he was sitting between two Brothers. They even put a cigarette between his lips. Till the moment of arrival, he was constantly thinking of those three words: Laid, harvest, pearls. He could not remember at all. They removed his blindfold right in front of his house. He even waved a hand. A woman wearing a black dress and a black scarf was walking in the street. Nobody was in. Plastic covered the angel. When he opened the door to the hallway, he pulled out his watch. He had to see. He had to read. He took off his sweater and smelled it. It no longer had that smell. He didn't feel like taking off the black shirt. After all, didn't he have to go to Amir Khan's Memorial in the afternoon? He pulled an overcoat or something over his shoulder, and went to the basement. The shelves were empty, but the desk, and even the chair were right where they used to be, and *The Seven Beauties*, too, was at the center of the desk, closed, but surely with a pencil in the middle. He had just begun reading these three lines.

I laid my head upon the pillow (there),
    and clasped that beauty tightly to my breast.
A harvest mine, with rose-decked willow white
    soft, delicate and lovely, white and pink.
A vision of a precious pearl within the shell;
    I gazed upon it and took her treasure for my own. [47]

---

47. C. E. Wilson, the English translator of Nizami's poem, found this line of poetry a bit too erotic and thus, in the style of other English translators of that period, chose to translate the line into Latin. The English translation is mine.

There was a noise at the door. Sarmad surely knew. That's what he had been reading when he started the commotion. Who was it? Let them come in, whoever they are. Farkhondeh and the kids have their own keys, and the others are oblivious to locks. It was his Mah and right behind her, Zohre, both wearing black dresses and scarves.

Mah said, "Is that you Dad? When did you come?"

Zohre was weeping. "What happened Dad?" she asked.

He wanted to say it had lasted only an hour, nothing to weep about. He didn't. The nice thing about these scarves and dresses was that with them, one could go straight to Amir Khan's Memorial. His Zohreh, pointing to his hair, began to weep. He took her purse, pulled out her small mirror. In this black shirt, how many years, how many centuries must have passed for his hair to have turned, one by one, so completely white.

Translator's Afterword

"He has two antagonists: the first presses him from behind, from the origin. The second blocks the road ahead. He gives battle to both. To be sure, the first supports him in his fight with the second, for he wants to push him forward, and in the same way, the second supports him in his fight with the first, since he drives him back. But it is only theoretically so. For it is not only the two antagonists who are there, but he himself as well, and who really knows his intentions? His dream, though, is that some time in an unguarded moment—and this would require a night darker than any night has ever been yet—will jump out of the fighting line and be promoted, on account of his experience in fighting, to the position of umpire over his antagonists in their fight with each other."

Kafka

Several months ago, I received an anonymous envelope from Iran. It contained several apparently random pages of a hand-written manuscript. In a few days, the mystery was more or less solved. By then I had received several other envelopes that ultimately completed all of the missing pages of what turned out to be a novella called *King of the Benighted*. A bulky package containing all the pages of the manuscript would surely have invited the ever-watchful gaze of the Islamic censors. Ironically then, part of what the author wished to convey was already contained in all the strategies of concealment and mutilation to which the manuscript had been, by necessity, subjected.

One envelope also contained a note, from the author. He wrote of his desire to see his work published anonymously in

English and asked for my help.

I found *King of the Benighted* to be a masterpiece both in form and content; a novella that successfully uses modern techniques of fiction superimposed upon the background of a rich tradition of Iranian prose and poetry. It shows the vitality and stylistic sophistication of modern Iranian fiction as well as the richness of its literary legacy. To use Eliot's words, here tradition and individual talent have complemented each other well to create a fine work of art. The author has creatively used treasures of past literature to blend with calamities of contemporary reality in Iran to sketch, in a modern, innovative style, a moving account of life under the Islamic Republic and a philosophical contemplation on the essence of Iran's historical past. *King of the Benighted* portrays the tragedy of the life of an artist living in a society where the pillars of the status quo, as well as the ideologues of the opposition, both wish to instrumentalize art and deny its aesthetic autonomy. In fact, what they both share is disdain for artistic and intellectual liberty, thus vulgarly "politicizing" all thinking and creativity. They both undermine "mediations" in art and society, submerging art into the expediencies of the political struggle and fostering a cult of political debunking. Consequently, many aspiring political cadres, bent on seizing power, have been forced into the ranks of artists, purveying their political wares in the guise of art, blurring the boundaries between art and political propaganda. The tragedy of political oppression, then, is not limited to the lives it destroys or the bodies it maims or mutilates. Equally tragic is the havoc imposed on the life of the mind and its aesthetic urges. In such an era, benighted indeed are those who become victims of apocalyptic ideas and utopian idealism. And then they, like the poet depicted in the story, become frighteningly lonely, mistrusted by the powers that be, misused by the opposition, and misunderstood by the populace. While in Rilke's words, "works of art are of an infinite solitude"[1] in societies such as Iran, where oppression stifles all aesthetic preoccupations, a poet or writer, like the narrator or the hero of *King of the Benighted*, committed to the aesthetic, and not instrumentalized values of his work, becomes tragically lonely.

King of the Benighted is, in spite of its overt, persistent political discourse and the grim reality it depicts, a literary manifesto for art as aesthetics and for artists who wish to free themselves from the straightjacket of self-righteous ideologies of Left or Right. In a sense, by both its form and content, the story epitomizes what can be considered a budding cultural and artistic revolution in Iranian society. This revolution has been flourishing in spite of the Islamic Regime's persistent attempts to stifle "non-Islamic" culture and art. Feigned shortages of paper; strict censorship where every book must receive a "license" from the "Ministry of Guidance," an Orwellian misnomer for sure; punitive governmental price control on undesirable books; repeated purges of artists and intellectuals from their educational and research posts; and a general official climate of anti-intellectualism have all been elements of the regime's pursuit of cultural domination. Yet in the social smithy of these developments, a new spirit has been forging. Iranian intellectuals, once filled with a Promethean sense of social and self-esteem, have now been driven to the spiritual and social suffering of a Pariah. Many dreams have turned into night-

---

1. Rilke, Rainer Maria. *Letters to a Young Poet*. tr. by Stephen Mitchell. N.Y. 1987. 23.

mares; many ideological icons have lost their sacred halo. A "revaluation of values" has indeed become the order of the day. A belated process of soul searching has begun. In social analysis, formulas retrieved from moldy attics of premolded ideological structures no longer seem attractive and convincing. In literary production, reception, and criticism, a subtle process of change is underway. While for many years literary theory was thought to be synonymous with social criticism, a genuine aesthetic discourse seems nascent. In fact, social realism, once sacrosanct in its banal Zhadanovian version, has lost its legitimacy. Iranian periodicals inside and outside Iran are replete with artistic and theoretical aspects of this cultural change. *King of the Benighted* can well be considered an excellent representative of aesthetic thinking that was previously thought only marginal but has now come to enjoy much more legitimacy in the Iranian literary milieu.

The novella is also a eulogy to utopia. It laments the loss of historical innocence. It decries an era that by the sheer force of its calumny impels artists to delve into the putrefying subjects of oppression, torture, and death: one that replaces the aura of artistic vitality with the grim odor of death.

Yet this aversion to the politics of oppression does not lead to purely depoliticized discourse or social passivity. Indeed, if we accept the notion that a text's epistemology and form is ultimately a political posture on the nature of authority,[2] then *King of the Benighted* delegitimizes traditional structures (and authorities) and posits alternative forms of thought and power.

---

2. Shapiro, Michael. "Literary Production as a Politicizing Practice." *Language and Politics*. Ed. by Michael Shapiro. N.Y. 1984. 215–255.

A case in point is what the story entails in terms of the relationship between the reader and the text. *King of the Benighted* is not easy reading. The author obviously does not see fiction as sheer *entertainment* or as part of the *culture industry*, wherein the demands of the market and the dictums of the assumed lowest common denominator of reader intelligence become the ultimate standard of acceptable artistic innovation and, in consequence, "easy" texts are legitimized at the expense of more formally demanding works.

Furthermore, in *King of the Benighted* art is in itself salvation and not an instrument of other messianic agendas. The author is free by the mere force of having told the story. Not only in the beginning was the word, at the end too there is nothing other than the word, and though the word is no longer the light, yet in its infinite realm of creativity lies the utopia immune from the onslaught of the apocalyptic visionaries or despotic dogmatists and the executioner they invariably bring; in it lies the only flicker of hope in an otherwise hopeless and tragic world.

In the story, a man, a poet by vocation, wakes up and finds nothing around him save images of death. Looking at the relics of the dead, he remembers moments in the life of Amir Khan, whose memorial he must attend in the afternoon.

At ten-thirty in the morning, he sets out to do his chores of the day. While haunting images of reality crowd his memory, his single source of solace is in the world of imagination. In particular, he remembers a poem by Nizami, the tale of the *King of the Benighted*: a eulogy for a lost utopia.

Upon his return home, he seems to receive unwanted visitors. They take him away. Memories of his past visit to prison, his poetry readings, and the disdain of the "comrades" for anything other than "committed art" come alive. And again, this time, to comfort and console those who share his fate in the cell, he recites poetry and tells them about the travails of the *King of the Benighted*.

His companion for much of the time is Sarmad. A moving account of his horrifying life forms the core of the latter half of the novella.

The poet returns home at eleven-thirty in the morning and remembers Amir Khan, whose memorial he must attend in the afternoon.

Throughout all of this, the author's style of narative is not simple or linear. Instead, from elements of present reality, personal memories, literary images, and historical facts, often crosscutting from one to the other with the atemporal and nonspatial liberties of human memory, he weaves a masterful tapestry that offers glimpses into the life of a creative mind in mindless times. The ominous reality of the external world, the two Kafkaesque antagonists that torment him, the "litter of reality" from which, according to Akmatova, poems are made, forces him more and more into the labyrinth of the mind. The use of such a technique lets him transform the agonies of his age and personal existence into something at once historical and imaginary.

The narrative paradigm of the author seems to be historical and personal mnemonics. With its power he becomes privy to the secrets of Iran's cultural past as well as the frightening spectre of its present reality. Mnemonics for him is also a means of bringing structure into a chaotic stream of consciousness. Images from his consciousness are thus interspersed with conjured figures from Iran's history, not only bringing order to the chaotic flow of the poets' immediate memory but also impregnating them with the collective historic character and consciousness of a land. The result is a "perception not only of the pastness of the past, but of its presence."[3]

The language of this mnemonic paradigm is often metaphoric and always as historically expansive as the subject it wishes to cover. While *King of the Benighted* in a sense recounts moments in the life of a contemporary poet, yet the life of that poet is itself a metaphor for the plight of all poets and creative and critical minds in the history of a land ruled by intolerance. To escape the narrow confines of Procrustean censorship and instrumentalized art and to articulate the timelessness of the story, the author expands the language of his narrative across the span of a millennium of Iranian prose and poetry. The essential linguistic and formal strategy of the text then has poetry, so singularly important in Iran's past, as its central metaphoric core and a style of prose both archaic and contemporary.

If the textual context of words are what give them their "metaphoric twist," then the context of this author's metaphors are not only the text itself, but the totality of Iran's cultural context. In other words, while in a freer society, metaphor and trope arise out of the open possibilities of the lexicon and a hermeneutic tradition that constantly attempts to uncover and expand new horizons above and below the word and the text, in closed societies, such as Iran's, the closed claustrophobic space of legitimate discourse forces language more and more

---

3. Eliot, T.S. *Points of View.* N.Y. 1931. 25.

into the realm of the metaphor. In this particular instance, the dense cultural and historical allusions that help form the "context" of the metaphors contribute to the difficulty in understanding them, particularly for non-Iranian readers. I hope the footnotes will partially help mitigate this problem.

In that spirit, a prose rendition of Nizami's long poem that constitutes the central metaphor for the story has been provided as a prologue. I have kept the notes to a minimum, hoping to save the narrative flow of the novella. After all, in spite of all cultural differences, in the final analysis, languages are not strangers to one another, but are, "apriori and apart from all historical relationship interrelated in what they want to express."[4]

A literal translation of the original title of this novella would be *King of Those Clad in Black* or *King of The Ebony-clad*; with a bit of "translator's license" and with the blessing of the author, I opted for *King of The Benighted*. At the same time in compliance with the author's wish to remain anonymous, and because in recent years many works by different authors living inside Iran have been published abroad under the common pen name of Manuchehr Irani, I chose the same name for the unkown author.

Many friends were kind enough to critically read parts or all of this manuscript. Ruth and Parviz Shokat, Helen Cradock, Ardavan Davaran, Leo Hamilian, Shirley Morrisson, Jean Mach, Barbara McDougall, and Kevin Maxwell all read the complete novella and made many inspiring suggestions. In particular, I

---

4. Benjamin, Walter. "The Task of the Translator." *Illuminations*. Ed. by Hannah Arendt. tr. by Harry Zohn. N.Y. 1968. 72.

wish to thank David Brostoff who generously gave of his time and used his meticulous and poetic sensitivity to words in helping me overcome many of the hurdles in rendering the novella into English. I am also indebted to Joanne Kaczor and Carol Bowen of the College of Notre Dame for help in typing parts of the manuscript.

The translation I dedicate to my son, Hamid, who I hope will live in a better millennium than the one described in this novella.

ABBAS MILANI
College of Notre Dame
Belmont, California

MANUCHEHR IRANI is a pen name used by many writers living in Iran and publishing their work abroad. The author is considered by his peers as the best contemporary Persian short story writer. *King of the Benighted*, written after the Revolution, is his first work to be translated and initially published in English under a pseudonym.

ABBAS MILANI belongs to a new generation of Iranian intellectuals, now living abroad, who have worked in Iran before, during and after the Revolution. Dr. Milani lives in California, where he is chairman of the Department of Social Science at the College of Notre Dame, Belmont.

NASRIN RAHIMIEH is assistant professor and Canada Research Fellow at the University of Alberta. She has published a book on Middle Eastern writers in exile and is completing a second on Persian travellers.

A NOTE ON THE TYPE

The text of this book was set in a digitized version of Janson, a typeface long thought to have been made by the Dutchman Anton Janson, who was a practicing type founder in Leipzig during the years 1668–1687. However, it has been conclusively demonstrated that these types are actually the work of Nicholas Kis (1650–1702), a Hungarian, who most probably learned his trade from the master Dutch type founder Dirk Voskens.

The type is an excellent example of the influential and sturdy Dutch types that prevailed in England.